preventing WORKPLACE BULLYING

Workplace bullying is more common and costly than most people realise. It can make life unbearable for employees in any industry, and ultimately undermine an organization's potential for profit. In this practical guide, Carlo Caponecchia and Anne Wyatt explain how to identify workplace bullying and apply best practice to preventing and managing it.

Caponecchia and Wyatt outline what constitutes bullying at work, demystify some of the controversial issues, and discuss the various factors which influence workplace bullying. The responsibilities of management, and legal implications are outlined, and supported with best practice guides for policies, complaints procedures and risk management systems. Options and resources for targets experiencing bullying are also explored. These ideas and concepts are illustrated throughout with real case studies.

This evidence-based book on workplace bullying is a valuable resource for organizations of all sizes and for anyone affected by bullying at work including employees, human resource managers, workplace consultants, counsellors, mediators and legal advisors.

Carlo Caponecchia is a Lecturer at the University of New South Wales, Australia. He is an expert in psychological hazards at work, and has conducted research and consultancy projects on bullying with several organisations.

Anne Wyatt has over 30 years of experience as an academic, expert advisor, consultant, trainer and speaker in the occupational health and safety and management fields.

CARLO CAPONECCHIA
& ANNE WYATT

preventing
WORKPLACE
BULLYING

An evidence-based guide for managers and employees

Routledge
Taylor & Francis Group

LONDON AND NEW YORK

First published in Australia in 2011
By Allen & Unwin Pty Ltd

First published in the UK in 2011
by Routledge
27 Church Road, Hove, East Sussex BN3 2FA

Simultaneously published in the USA and Canada
by Routledge
711 Third Avenue, New York NY 10017

Routledge is an imprint of the Taylor & Francis Group, an Informa business

British Library Cataloguing in Publication Data
A catalogue record for this book is available from the British Library

Library of Congress Cataloging in Publication Data
Caponecchia, Carlo.
  Preventing workplace bullying : an evidence-based guide for managers and
employees / Carlo Caponecchia and Anne Wyatt. – 1st ed.
      p. cm.
  Includes bibliographical references and index.
  ISBN 978-0-415-66880-4 (hardback) – ISBN 978-0-415-66881-1 (pbk.) 1. Bullying
in the workplace. 2. Bullying in the workplace–Prevention. I. Wyatt, Anne. II. Title.
  BF637.B85C37 2011
  658.3'045–dc22
                                  2010049138

ISBN: 978-0-415-66880-4 (hbk)
ISBN: 978-0-415-66881-1 (pbk)
ISBN: 978-0-203-81480-2 (ebk)

Text and paperback cover design by Melissa Keogh
Typeset in 10.5/16pt Birka by Midland Typesetters, Australia
Printed and bound in Great Britain by TJ International, Padstow, Cornwall

CONTENTS

ACKNOWLEDGEMENTS

In addition to the support and patience of our families and friends, we are very grateful to the following people who have provided assistance in producing this book, through offering advice and sharing their experience and insight.

Cathy Butcher; Siobhán Cantrill, Meagan Crisp; Judith Daley; Dwight Dowda; Benjamin Dodds; Maria Ferrara; Dianne Gardner; Elisa Ilarda; Francesco Lo Pizzo; David Marks; Chondona O'Brien; Libby Permazel; Charlotte Rayner; Leanne Tasker; Ross Underwood; Patricia Villaroel; Stacey Weeks; Trudy Wilson; Elizabeth Weiss; Amanda Wishaw and Jim Wyatt.

part one

WHAT IS WORKPLACE BULLYING?

CHAPTER 1. WHAT IS WORKPLACE BULLYING?

Before we get started

Before we enter the world of workplace bullying, we want to provide a note on our approach and the terms we use. You will notice as you read this book that we usually refrain from using words such as 'bully' or 'victim'. This is not because we're trying to be politically correct, but it goes to the heart of our approach to unacceptable behaviours at work. These behaviours have significant negative effects on people. We view preventing them as part of the responsibilities that we have to each other regarding safety and wellbeing in the workplace. One of the core values in workplace safety is that we don't simply blame individuals, but rather, we look for systemic factors that could have influenced the occurrence of a negative event. Of course, individuals are still responsible for their own behaviour and play an important role in what happens, but the interaction between the person, the situation and the system is also important. This approach is supported in various domains, such as when explaining the torture and abuse of prisoners that occurred in Abu Ghraib (see Zimbardo 2007).

Our language should reflect our values. The term 'bully' implies that the problem is completely the individual—and in some cases the individual is a large part of the problem—but what about the workplace culture that allows that behaviour to continue? The term 'victim' has similar problems; it infers helplessness on the part of the person experiencing unacceptable behaviours. Thus we try to take a balanced approach. This book is neither pro-'victim' or pro-'bully'. Unacceptable behaviours can be very harmful for *everyone* involved. We need to minimise the harm that could happen to the 'victim' and/or the alleged 'bully' when unacceptable behaviours are poorly managed. We'll talk more about these issues throughout the book, but for now, it's important to say that generally:

- instead of calling someone a 'bully', we refer to their behaviour as the 'person who uses bullying behaviours'; and
- instead of calling someone a 'victim', we refer to them as 'targets' or 'targets of bullying behaviour'.

As far as practicable, we have taken an evidence-based approach to the topic of workplace bullying. That means we have prioritised current, peer-reviewed research and literature above collected case experience or accounts from people who have perceived that they have been targeted by workplace bullying behaviours. A range of types of evidence have been used, because different sources of evidence are appropriate for answering different questions. It is early days in terms of workplace bullying research and there are still many gaps in knowledge and understanding in the field. Throughout the book we have acknowledged the evidence that we have used so it can be referred to and used by our readers.

Definitions of workplace bullying

Bullying is seen as a psychological hazard at work. It is best thought of as a potential stressor—a cause of stress (Rayner 1998). This means that it has all the usual consequences of stress. The starting point of any discussion of workplace bullying has to be what it is and what it is not. This information is really important, and forms the basis of all the other topics we will consider in later chapters, including what we can do about bullying if it is happening in our workplace, and what we can do if it is happening to us.

While use of the term 'workplace bullying' is increasing, people can use the term without knowing exactly what it means, or use it to mean several different things at different times. It is important that we are all speaking the same language before we continue talking about workplace bullying and what to do about it.

Reading the scientific literature on workplace bullying doesn't always help, because scientists are also using several terms, and sometimes they are used interchangeably. When we step back from all the different terms and their usage, however, and look at the trends regarding what bullying is thought to be, a much clearer picture emerges. The main criteria for behaviour to be called workplace bullying are that the behaviours:

- are repeated,
- unreasonable, and
- cause harm, or have the potential to cause harm (Einarsen et al. 2003; WorkSafe Victoria 2003; Caponecchia & Wyatt 2009).

Unreasonable behaviours

The types of behaviours that are often thought of as bullying, if they meet the other criteria, are behaviours such as:

- undue public criticism;
- name calling, insults or intimidation;
- social or physical isolation (which might also include witholding information or preventing access to opportunities);
- overwork (such as impossible deadlines, undue disruptions);
- destabilisation and undermining behaviour (for example, failure to give credit, assigning people meaningless tasks, setting people up to fail, reminding people of their mistakes, removing responsibility without cause);
- yelling and shouting;
- spreading malicious rumours and gossiping;
- repeated unreasonable assignment of duties which are obviously unfavourable to a particular individual; and
- witholding or denying access to necessary information, consultation or other resources (Rayner & Hoel 1997; CIPD 2005; WorkCover NSW 2008; WorkSafe Victoria 2003; Irish Health and Safety Authority 2001).

The development of a definitive list of behaviours that constitute bullying has been abandoned by researchers in the field. This is due to the many different ways in which bullying can manifest, and also because bullying can include both acts of commission and acts of omission, which by their nature are hard to define and identify (Rayner 2007). We will talk more about the subtle nature of some bullying behaviours in Chapter 3.

Box 1.1 What's in a name? 'Bullying' versus 'mobbing'

The terms 'bullying' and 'mobbing' are sometimes used to mean similar things, and sometimes quite different things. The word 'mobbing' originates from a phenomenon observed in bird behaviour. Birds often gang up on predators, or other animals that are regarded as a threat, protecting themselves and the group (Royal Society for the Protection of Birds 2001).

Leymann (1990), one of the original mobbing researchers, defined mobbing as 'hostile and unethical communication which is directed in a systematic way *by one or a number of persons* mainly toward one individual' (p. 120, italics added). In other locations, however, 'mobbing' was used to only refer to situations where groups of people enact particular negative behaviours on others. This second usage seems reasonable, given the clear connotation of group behaviour that 'mobbing' has in English.

These differences in usage would not be a problem, except for the tendency that people have to use 'bullying' and 'mobbing' interchangeably, or use 'bullying/mobbing' without stating exactly what they mean. This has created confusion and made comparison of different research findings problematic. Leymann (2000) suggested that we use 'bullying' for schoolyard behaviours, and 'mobbing' for workplace behaviours, but this has not really been taken up.

The main difference that exists between the use of 'bullying' and 'mobbing' is the reference to individual versus group-based behaviour respectively. Theorists have attempted to argue for various other distinctions between the terms (e.g. Bultena & Whatcott 2008; Westhues 2008), but there is little scientific evidence for this.

We use 'bullying' to refer to repeated unreasonable behaviours used by one person towards another; and we use 'mobbing', more specifically, to refer to repeated unreasonable behaviours used by a group towards an individual (or group). There is evidence to suggest that unacceptable behaviours are often perpetrated by more than one individual towards a target (Rayner &

Daley 2010). Most of the information in this book will apply to mobbing as well as bullying. The effects of unacceptable behaviours on the individual and the organisation, the processes that organisations should employ to prevent and manage the behaviours, and the strategies targets could adopt will be largely the same for mobbing and bullying.

What is unreasonable?

The definition of what is 'unreasonable' essentially relies on the legally constructed 'reasonable person test'. This refers to whether a hypothetical reasonable person, taking account of the relevant circumstances, would consider the behaviour to be reasonable or not.

Reasonableness is sometimes seen as a problematic aspect of workplace bullying, because people often cite that it depends on a person's perception. It is difficult to determine what is reasonable or unreasonable when you think you may be the target of some of the behaviours outlined above. It may be useful to discuss the circumstances with other people—friends, family, colleagues, or someone independent of the situation who can be relied on to be somewhat impartial—in order to gain an external perspective on whether the behaviour seems to be reasonable or not.

An assessment of (un)reasonableness in the absence of clear guidelines on workplace bullying can lead to over-reporting and under-reporting. Organisations can help to define what behaviours are acceptable or unacceptable in their policies and procedures, and we will talk more about what organisations and individuals can do about bullying in Part 3.

Frequency and duration of the behaviours

Whilst a single instance of unreasonable workplace behaviour is typically not considered bullying, single incidents may still be hazardous. In addition, the single incident may form part of a series of behaviours that, retrospectively considered, could constitute bullying. It is important to note single incidents because they alert us to the occurrence of unacceptable behaviours. In saying that the unreasonable behaviours must be 'repeated', we need to then consider their frequency. How often is often enough to be considered bullying? When researchers first started thinking about workplace bullying, behaviours were thought to have to occur weekly for six months in order for them to be considered part of an overall bullying pattern (Leymann 1990). This criterion has been replaced by the less stringent guideline that the behaviours have to be regular rather than occasional (Einarsen et al. 2003). This new guideline is appropriate because assigning a definitive number of instances per time period is somewhat artificial—what happens if the behaviour happens twice in one week, does not occur for two weeks, and then re-occurs three weeks later? We may still want to call this behaviour bullying.

There is no easy way of establishing such duration criteria, because what is acceptable or unreasonable as a 'duration criterion' may well depend on the circumstances (such as the degree of contact that groups of people have with each other). We would suggest that if the behaviours are repeatedly experienced to the extent that they cause repeated offense, distress, humiliation or embarrassment, then at the very least the behaviours should be assessed. This 'assessment' may occur with or by a colleague, a manager or human resources representative, or an external person who is appropriately qualified. Many would argue that the target's own perspective on the behaviour is the most important consideration in determining whether the behaviour has occurred for 'long enough'. If a person feels there is a problem, then, at some level, there is a problem that needs to be investigated. Of course, the behaviours may or may not be bullying. The importance of recognising when behaviours constitute bullying or some other kind of unacceptable behaviour(s) is an extremely important issue, and is dealt with in detail in Chapter 2. Hopefully, increasing awareness of workplace bullying and related behaviours will serve to (a) reduce bullying from happening, and (b) make people more aware of what bullying is, what it is not, and accordingly, when to act.

Potential to cause harm

A hazard is 'a source of potential harm'. People are familiar with hazards such as poisons, harmful micro-organisms or moving machinery. Only over the last few decades have 'psychological' hazards been seriously considered in the workplace context. Broadly, psychological hazards are those which lead to stress responses and other psychological symptoms, and arise from factors such as working long hours, undertaking rotating shiftwork, work overload and low levels of control over one's work.

In addition, since the mid-1990s, certain *behaviours* have been considered hazardous. Nowadays, collectively, such behaviours are often termed 'unacceptable behaviours'. The use of bullying behaviour, which is an example of unacceptable workplace behaviour, is now considered to be a workplace psychological hazard. It is possible that in some contexts behaviours that seem like bullying do not cause harm, or have negative effects. Causing harm, or having the potential to cause harm is an important inclusion in the workplace bullying concept because it helps identify situations that are most serious.

As well as identifying hazards in the workplace there is a need to think in terms of the 'risk' presented by the hazards and the ways in which the risks may be controlled. Risk is generally considered in terms of the likelihood and consequences of harm being caused by exposure to the hazard, depending on the context in which the hazard exists.

Risk is not the same as 'hazard', contrary to what some people think. Risk is 'the chance of something happening that will have an impact on objectives' (Standards Australia 2009) that may be presented by a hazard. So, when we think about risk we need to think in terms of the hazard itself and the context in which the hazard occurs. For example, if we think about the hazard presented by moving machinery, the risk is greater if controls such as machine guards are not in place. Similarly, if workplace bullying goes unchecked in a workplace (the context), and is allowed to escalate, the risk (the likelihood of negative consequences) of the hazard is greater. In terms of priorities, it is the higher risk situations that need to be managed first.

This book takes a 'risk management' perspective on the workplace hazard of bullying behaviours. Thus, it considers ways in which risk reduction in relation to the hazard of bullying behaviours may occur.

Box 1.2 Did they really mean it?

The question of intention is a controversial one in workplace bullying. Some researchers believe that the behaviour needs to be intentional to be considered to be bullying (see Keashly 1998 for the centrality of intent in defining workplace abuse), while others allow for bullying to be either intentional or unintentional (Richards & Daley 2003).

There are three main problems with *requiring* intention for behaviour to be considered bullying:

1. It is very difficult to assess intention, especially when the nature of bullying behaviours can be such that they can be disguised, or occur 'under the radar'. Requiring intent effectively puts further burden on the target of the behaviours to provide evidence of someone else's motivational state.

2. Given the difficulties in proving intention, lots of behaviours that affect people in a negative manner could simply be ignored because intention cannot be proved, and thus the behaviour could not be labelled 'bullying'.

3. Requiring intention as part of the definition of bullying can give people (and organisations) an easy defence: 'I never meant it'. This is inappropriate when it is clear that in some cases bullying behaviours are carefully planned and executed.

Accordingly, it seems more reasonable to think that bullying behaviours could be either intentional or unintentional.

Power imbalance

The idea of a power imbalance between the individuals involved in workplace bullying is sometimes included in definitions of workplace bullying, and in other instances is omitted (for example, WorkSafe Victoria 2003; WorkCover NSW 2008; CIPD 2005). There are two possible reasons for not including power imbalance in definitions of bullying. The first is that it is so obvious there is a power imbalance between the individuals involved that it is implied, and does not really add to the definition. The second reason is that there is a danger that definitions may imply that workplace bullying is only enacted by a superior upon a subordinate.

Power imbalance is an important consideration in workplace bullying, because it can help us understand the processes of what has occurred between the individuals involved. This may be particularly important should the events be investigated or some other type of resolution attempted.

Power is variously defined, though modern notions recognise that it is not just the capability to influence others but the potential for influence. In the context of workplace bullying, power needs to be understood more widely than traditional superior/subordinate relationships. There are many potential bases of power that may be used in bullying relationships, including age, time with the organisation, experience in particular tasks/roles, personal relationships (such as being a friend of the manager), or other forms of social power (see Salin 2003).

The following is a good example of a non-hierarchical power base being used to bully others:

> Joan is responsible for organising venues and catering for meetings and events in a large public sector organisation. She is very skilled at public relations and often joins in on the social aspects of the events, gaining 'behind-the-scenes' knowledge of the politics of the organisation. She amassed a high degree of social power, despite being at a relatively low level of the organisational hierarchy, because she knew everybody's business: who was attending particular meetings, who was organising them, and what was happening in their personal lives. She could choose to divulge or withhold this information, or make it a little more 'juicy', as she wished. Malicious rumors and gossip were frequently started and perpetuated by Joan.

Of course, there is ample evidence that bullying does occur from superior to subordinate (Einarsen et al. 2003). As Salin (2003) indicates, hierarchical power has been shown to give rise to bullying, as bullying is prevalent in military and service organisations which emphasise rigid hierarchical structures. However, we also know that bullying occurs from subordinates to superiors. This has been termed 'upwards bullying' (Branch et al. 2007). The notion of power imbalances can add a richness to our understanding of the ways in which workplace bullying can occur but it needs to be viewed in a broad manner, rather than just as traditional hierarchical power.

What if the behaviour doesn't seem to meet the criteria for bullying?

As suggested above, some of the expectations regarding features of bullying behaviours, which identify them as bullying, rely to a degree on perception and circumstance. It is not easy to make a determination about whether something is bullying or not without considering all the information and the context in which the behaviour occurred. If behaviours that are causing harm are occurring less frequently than suggested above, or otherwise do not meet the criteria for bullying, that doesn't mean the behaviours should be tolerated. Several possibilities exist. The behaviours could:

- be bullying distributed across several targets, all of whom have not individually experienced bullying behaviours frequently enough or for long enough for the behaviour to meet the criteria (see Box 1.3);
- be harassment, discrimination, violence, conflict, or some combination of these. These are related to, but distinct from, bullying;
- represent poor workplace behaviour. Behaviours that do not meet the criteria for bullying, harassment, discrimination and violence can still be offensive, and have a significant effect on the individuals involved.

In all these instances it is important to treat reports of unacceptable behaviour as serious, seek more information on how to 'diagnose' them, and deal with them appropriately.

Box 1.3 Case study: Code of Conduct

This case is an example of where bullying behaviours were used across several employees in a workplace. The case also shows that robust codes of conduct can result in the removal of individuals who use bullying behaviours from the work environment.

Geoffrey Purser v Commonwealth Attorney PR932560 [2003] AIRC 615 (5 June 2003)

A senior legal officer employed by the Commonwealth Attorney General's Department was dismissed for breaching the Australian Public Service (APS)

Code of Conduct which required that: 'An APS employee, when acting in the course of APS employment, must treat everyone with respect and courtesy, and without harassment'.

Evidence was given that the senior legal officer had used physically and verbally abusive behaviour towards staff on many occasions. His behaviour included pushing, use of an aggressive posture, yelling, unreasonably criticising work performance and refusing to delegate and transfer files to another legal officer.

The senior legal officer claimed that his dismissal had been unfair. The Australian Industrial Relations Commission found that his dismissal had been valid.

After hearing all the evidence, Commissioner Deegan concluded (at paragraph 119 of the judgment), 'I have set out a great deal of the evidence in this matter so as to indicate the seriousness of the behaviour claimed to constitute the breach of the APS Code of Conduct. Any failure to treat a person or a fellow employee with "courtesy and respect" could conceivably constitute a breach of the Code. Many such breaches would not incur a sanction of termination of employment. In the applicant's case there were numerous, in my view serious, failures to comply with the requirement of subsection 13(3) of the *Public Service Act 1999*, to treat people with respect and courtesy . . .'

Commissioner Deegan made the following determination (at paragraph 134):

> It is regrettable that the applicant's conduct was allowed to affect staff for such a period. It is clear that Ms E and Ms P attempted to curb his behaviour when it was brought to their attention. The fact that several employees believed they would suffer retribution if their complaints were brought to the applicant's attention hampered earlier action by Ms P and Ms E. I accept that the delay also resulted from their desire to be scrupulously fair to the applicant in dealing with the matters brought to their attention.

The case was appealed, though the appeal was unsuccessful.

(Source: http://www.austlii.edu.au/cgi-bin/sinodisp/au/cases/cth/AIRC/ 2003/615.html?query=title(Geoffrey%20Purser) accessed 9 March 2008)

References

Branch, S., Ramsay, S. & Barker, M. 2007, Managers in the firing line: Contributing factors to workplace bullying by staff—an interview study, *Journal of Management and Organisation, 13*, 264–81.

Bultena, C.D. & Whatcott, R.B. 2008, Bushwacked at work: A comparative analysis of mobbing and bullying at work. Paper presented at the American Society of Business and Behavioural Sciences.

Caponecchia, C. & Wyatt, A. 2009, Distinguishing between bullying, harassment and violence: A risk management approach, *Journal of Occupational Health and Safety Australia and New Zealand, 25*(6), 439–449.

CIPD 2005, *Bullying at work: Beyond policies to a culture of respect*, London: Chartered Institute of Personnel Development.

Einarsen, S., Hoel, H., Zapf, D. & Cooper, C.L. 2003, The concept of bullying at work: The European tradition, in S. Einarsen, H. Hoel, D. Zapf & C.L. Cooper (Eds.), *Bullying and Emotional Abuse in the Workplace: International perspectives in research and practice* (1st ed., pp. 3–30), London: Taylor & Francis.

Irish Health and Safety Authority 2001, Dignity at Work: The challenge of workplace bullying, Dublin: Irish Health and Safety Authority.

Keashly, L. 1998, Emotional abuse in the workplace: Conceptual and empirical issues, *Journal of Emotional Abuse, 1*(1), 85–117.

Leymann, H. 1990, Mobbing and psychological terror at workplaces, *Violence and Victims, 5*, 119–26.

—— 2000, The Mobbing encyclopaedia, retrieved 15 November 2008, from http://www.leymann.se/English/frame.html

Rayner, C. 1998, Workplace bullying: Do something! *Journal of Occupational Health and Safety Australia and New Zealand, 14*, 581–5.

—— 2007, Preparing for dignity: Tackling indignity at work, in S.C. Bolton (Ed.), *Dimensions of Dignity at Work*: Butterworth Heinemann pp. 176–90.

Rayner, C. & Daley, H. 2010, Are we getting anywhere? The British public sector twelve years on: A comparative study 1997–2009. Paper presented at the 7th International Conference on Workplace Bullying and Harassment, June 2010, Cardiff, Wales.

Rayner, C. & Hoel, H. 1997, A summary review of literature relating to workplace bullying, *Journal of Community and Applied Social Psychology, 7*, 181–91.

Richards, J. & Daley, H. 2003, Bullying policy: Development, implementation and monitoring, in S. Einarsen, H. Hoel, D. Zapf & C.L. Cooper (Eds.), *Bullying and Emotional Abuse in the Workplace: International perspectives in research and practice* (1st ed., pp. 247–58), London: Taylor & Francis.

Royal Society for the Protection of Birds 2001, Mobbing, retrieved 15 November 2008, from http://www.rspb.org.uk/advice/watchingbirds/behaviour/mobbing.asp

Salin, D. 2003, Ways of explaining workplace bullying: A review of enabling, motivating and precipitating structures and processes in the work environment, *Human Relations,* 56(10), 1213–32.

Standards Australia 2009, Risk Management: principles and guidelines AS/NZs ISO 31000:2009, Sydney: Standards Australia/Standards New Zealand.

Westhues, K. 2008, Critiques of the anti-bullying movement and responses to them. Paper presented at the 6th International Conference on Workplace Bullying.

WorkCover NSW 2008, Preventing and dealing with workplace bullying: A guide for employers and employees: WorkCover NSW.

WorkSafe Victoria 2003, Guidance note on the prevention of bullying and violence at work, Melbourne: WorkSafe Victoria.

Zimbardo, P. 2007, *The Lucifer effect: How good people turn evil*, London: Rider Books.

CHAPTER 2. WHAT IS NOT WORKPLACE BULLYING?

Now that we have clarified what workplace bullying is, it's important to discuss what it is not. In this chapter we'll look at situations that should not be considered to be bullying. We'll also talk about other kinds of behaviours that are related to but are distinct from bullying, such as conflict, discrimination, harassment and violence.

False-positives and false-negatives

No-one working in this field, be they a researcher, practitioner, or involved in managing workplaces, wants people to report workplace bullying when it is not actually occurring. This is known as 'false-positive' reporting, or more colloquially, playing host to 'the boy who cried wolf'. False-positive reporting is costly, emotionally draining, and may create more of a problem than originally existed. On the other hand, we know that workplace bullying can be under-reported when it actually has happened, which we call 'false-negative'.

False-positive reporting of bullying can also occur when an accusation of bullying is used as retribution or payback, or as a deliberate attempt to undermine someone. These are sometimes known as 'vexatious' or 'malicious' claims. An example of a *false-positive claim based on inappropriate information* would be where an injured employee has attended workplace bullying training, and subsequently, when his return to work coordinator repeatedly reminds him to attend his medical appointments, he accuses her of bullying him. An example of a *vexatious claim, intended as retribution* would be where an employee falsely accuses her supervisor of bullying soon after she was disciplined by the supervisor for inappropriate use of company records.

False-negative reporting can occur when people do not realise they are being targeted by bullying behaviours when, in fact, they are. The 'Chair in the Warehouse' case is an example of a situation where, when questioned by witnesses, a young woman denied she was being targeted by bullying behaviour (see Box 2.1).

Box 2.1 The 'chair in the warehouse' case

A young female employee had returned to work following lengthy rehabilitation from a workplace accident. She had suffered severe spinal injuries. To assist her with pain management and posture, she had been prescribed a special orthopaedic chair which was quite expensive. After a short period, the young woman's chair 'disappeared' each night, and each morning she had to determine where it was and organise to have it returned to her. The employee was apparently unconcerned by this, stating, 'Well, obviously someone on the night shift finds the chair useful, which is good'.

Investigations that included the examination of CCTV footage showed that warehouse staff were removing the young woman's chair each night and 'hiding' it in various places around the building. Examination of emails between staff revealed that this was happening because some of the young woman's colleagues envied the special attention and the expensive equipment with which she had been supplied.

The perpetrators were confronted and strongly disciplined for their proven unacceptable behaviour.

False-positives and false-negatives can also occur if people don't have a clear understanding of what bullying is or don't know how to distinguish it from other kinds of behaviours. We need to give clear guidelines on how to recognise a problem, and how to recognise when something is not a problem. The potential for vexatious claims is an unfortunate consequence of raising understanding of the workplace bullying issue, but does not mean we can afford to ignore workplace bullying. We need to increase awareness of bullying while making sure this is tempered by a clear, rational and responsible understanding of bullying and the concepts to which it is related.

Behaviours that are not bullying

One of the few pieces of legislation that specifically defines both what bullying is and what it is not is the *South Australian Occupational Health, Safety and Welfare Act (1986)*. (Other relevant legislation is considered in Chapter 5.) In section 55A (2), the Act outlines that bullying does not include:

(a) reasonable action taken in a reasonable manner by an employer to transfer, demote, discipline, counsel, retrench or dismiss an employee; or

(b) a decision by an employer, based on reasonable grounds, not to award or provide a promotion, transfer, or benefit in connection with an employee's employment; or

(c) reasonable administrative action taken in a reasonable manner by an employer in connection with an employee's employment; or

(d) reasonable action taken in a reasonable manner under an Act affecting an employee.

Although this Act only applies in South Australia, it has frequently been used as a model definition of those managerial actions which do not constitute bullying. Deciding which behaviours are acceptable or unacceptable again hinges on the issue of 'reasonableness'. As we discussed in Chapter 1, reasonableness refers to what a reasonable person, having account of all the circumstances in the situation, would consider to be reasonable. For example, imagine that an employee has been repeatedly alerted to his observed under-performance, and subsequently claims to have been bullied. An assessment of whether the action taken was reasonable would involve knowing about the employee's performance in his work context. Assessment of whether this action could be considered to be bullying would involve knowing about the employee's performance, and about any other behaviours or events that may have occurred to form a pattern of repeated behaviours, which could then also be assessed for their reasonableness (for example, undue public criticism, removing the employee from email lists).

Criteria for what is not bullying can be extremely useful when constructing policy and procedure documents. When confronted with the topic of workplace bullying, managers often express the reservation that doing something about bullying will interfere with their ability to 'manage' their staff (that is, give feedback, assign tasks, execute difficult decisions). They may fear that they might be accused of bullying or be concerned about false-positive reports. These concerns are understandable. A clear, documented indication of what bullying is not can help resolve this issue.

Workplace 'psychopaths'

We've talked about reporting bullying when bullying is not occurring (false-positives), and not reporting bullying when it is occurring (false-negatives), but there are other kinds of inappropriate reporting. Mislabelling the behaviour, or overstating the nature or extent of what is happening, can be equally destructive.

One approach that falls into this trap, and is increasingly applied to workplace bullying, is the 'workplace psychopaths' approach (see Clarke 2005; Babiak & Hare 2006). The 'workplace psychopaths' approach claims that there are psychopaths in our workplaces, and estimates that about 1–3 per cent of the (general) population are psychopaths (Clarke 2005). The behaviour of psychopaths at work is described from a clinical perspective, and attempts are made to create typologies of different styles of workplace psychopath (Clarke 2005). The behaviour in which these people engage is horrendous, and is in some ways similar to bullying.

There certainly are people in the world who could appropriately be diagnosed as 'psychopathic'. To what extent they are in our workplaces, and whether they fit into a neat typology, is a matter for science, however. The real problem with this approach is its misapplication to workplace bullying (Caponecchia & Wyatt 2008).

This misapplication is a concern because the idea that there are psychopaths at work has become quite popular. 'Psychopath' is an emotive term that most people are familiar with. The idea that you could call someone in your workplace a 'psycho' is almost fun, and something that people probably already do in a jocular manner (Caponecchia & Wyatt 2007). The titles of some of the books that outline the 'workplace psychopaths' approach are similarly emotive, and include: *Working with Monsters: How to identify and protect yourself from the workplace psychopath*, Clarke (2005), and *Snakes in Suits: When psychopaths go to work*, Babiak & Hare (2006). Indeed, if the books are not enough, people can even take continuing education courses to further inform themselves about workplace psychopaths.

The approach is also popular because it provides people with a coping strategy for bad behaviour at work. Being able to label someone else as the problem is likely to make people feel better (Caponecchia & Wyatt 2008). Labelling someone as a 'psychopath,' however, constitutes one of the major shortcomings of this approach.

As outlined previously, our approach to workplace bullying is informed by the field of occupational health and safety and risk management. Bullying is viewed as a workplace hazard from which employers have a duty to protect their employees, in a similar manner to any other hazard, be it chemical, physical or biological. Just as individuals are not usually seen as the sole cause of a workplace accident, they should not be seen as the sole cause of a psychological hazard at work, such as workplace bullying. The workplace psychopaths approach is inconsistent with these values because it focuses on an issue that is intrinsic to a person—their personality. Focusing just on personality—extremely aberrant or otherwise—is misleading, and we'll talk more about why in Chapter 4. Some of the other problems with the workplace psychopaths approach, when it is applied to workplace bullying, are outlined below.

Problem 1. Blame and vilification

One of the side effects of blaming an individual is that it may end up vilifying them. They may have done nothing wrong, or they may have committed minor offences, which are not extreme enough to be objectively classified as 'psychopathic'. In cases such as this, stigmatising the individual by calling them a 'workplace psychopath' may have a significant negative impact on them, on their relationships at work, and their reputation (Caponecchia & Wyatt 2007, 2008).

Problem 2. Misdiagnosis

The books about workplace psychopaths, which promise the reader the ability to identify workplace psychopaths, do caution against the inappropriate use of diagnostic criteria. Only people who are appropriately qualified should be diagnosing others with psychopathy or related complaints. Nevertheless these books still provide lists of diagnostic criteria. It is naïve to expect that people reading this material will not try to 'diagnose' others, despite warnings to the contrary. Major newspapers have subsequently published five-point checklists to help people determine whether their boss is a 'psycho' (Silkstone 2007). The consequences of this, in terms of stigmatisation and vilification, are quite obvious. It should also be noted, that one cannot receive a diagnosis of 'psychopathy' under the current arrangements for diagnosis of mental disorders (APA 2000). The appropriateness of the diagnosis that is used for such individuals (antisocial personality disorder) remains a contentious issue (see Hare 1996; Hicklin & Widiger 2005).

Problem 3. Anyone can do it

The workplace psychopaths approach, by focusing on an aspect of personality, suggests that only certain people use bad behaviours at work. Anyone can use bullying behaviour at any time; not just the rare people who have a diagnosable personality disorder. On the flip side of this, just because someone displays bad behaviours at work doesn't mean they have a personality disorder, no matter how tempting it is to conclude that they do.

Problem 4. Implications for control strategies

The workplace psychopaths approach offers little in the way of control strategies for workplace bullying. Psychopaths are described as being 'sent to Coventry' (that is, moved to an isolated part of the organisation), or they leave and find another job. This just perpetuates the behaviours somewhere else. Moving people to new jobs or new organisations is not always the best solution, and in most cases it should not be the first solution. The workplace psychopaths approach, when applied to bullying, offers little in terms of prevention.

Taken together, these problems leave us questioning why we would use the workplace psychopaths approach at all when dealing with workplace bullying. For this reason, providing information about workplace psychopaths is important in outlining what workplace bullying is not. The above discussion highlights that though there are many topics that seem to be related to bullying, they are not necessarily one and the same. If new topics are to be added to workplace bullying, we need to be very careful and deliberate about defining how they relate. This idea is important in the following sections that examine other behaviours to which bullying is related.

What is bullying related to?

It would be nice if the field of workplace bullying was black and white, but the reality is, of course, far more complex than that. The word 'bullying' is often used in conjunction with several other terms, such as conflict, harassment and violence, and they can occur together. Sometimes these terms are used interchangeably, or categorised, directly or implicitly, as subcategories of one another (for example, bullying as a form of harassment, Hill 2006; bullying as a form of violence, Hockley 2002; Mayhew 2004; harassment as a form of bullying, Hadikin & O'Driscoll 2000; Stranks 2005). It is really important that we articulate how these concepts are related to one another, because far from being just semantic distinctions, the differences between the concepts require different awareness and management strategies (Caponecchia & Wyatt 2009).

Bullying and conflict

Unresolved or unmanaged conflict can escalate into workplace bullying (Einarsen 1999; Keashly & Nowell 2003). Extensive coverage of workplace conflict is beyond the scope of this book, but some examples of types of conflict that may occur in the workplace include:

- *interpersonal conflicts*—for example, based on rivalry between people such as where one promotion is available and a number of people have applied for it;
- *values-related conflicts*—for example, in relation to culture, ideology or work standards where people do not understand what is important to those with different values from their own;
- *information-related conflicts*—for example, where people are applying different meanings from the same information, or using information from different sources;
- *structural conflicts*—for example, where reporting lines are absent or not clearly defined and this is a source of tension between people; and
- *complex conflicts*—where various types of conflicts 'converge' (Condliffe 2008).

Appropriate early interventions may include counselling, facilitated conversations, training and education, clarification and in some cases, mediation. The latter involves an impartial third party assisting the conflicted parties to reach an agreement. In other cases, assistance from outside the organisation may be required. Where early intervention occurs, workplace bullying may be averted.

Bullying, discrimination and harassment

Bullying and harassment are two terms that are often used together (for example, in Parker 2008). Many organisations will have a 'bullying and harassment' policy, or will have added the word 'bullying' to their existing harassment policies, forming a 'harassment/bullying' policy. It is not always apparent that the differences between the two concepts are understood, or reflected in policies and procedures.

Based on what we have already discussed about workplace bullying in Chapter 1, the main criteria for behaviour to be considered bullying are that the behaviours are repeated and unreasonable; and cause, or have the potential to cause harm.

We need to keep these criteria in mind when discussing harassment and discrimination.

Bullying and discrimination

Discrimination means treating someone unfairly because they belong to a particular group of people (Anti-discrimination Board of New South Wales 2009). Discrimination can occur on the basis of one or more characteristics, including:

- sex
- homosexuality
- marital status
- age
- transgender status
- status as a carer
- race and ethno-religious background, or colour
- disability

(*New South Wales Anti-discrimination Act 1977*).

Information about discrimination and harassment is slightly different in each jurisdiction, so it is important to make sure you refer to the law and guidance material that applies in your area. See Box 2.2 for further discussion and resources on this issue.

To give an example, discrimination on the basis of sex is behaviour that on the grounds of sex:

- treats the aggrieved person less favourably than someone of the opposite sex, in the same circumstances; or
- requires the aggrieved person to comply with a requirement or condition which a higher proportion of people of the opposite sex are able to comply with, and the requirement is not reasonable with respect to the circumstances.

Requiring someone to be 180 centimetres tall in order to get a job could be sexual discrimination (unless being that tall is really necessary to perform that job) because fewer women will be able to comply with that requirement than men (Anti-discrimination Board of New South Wales 2005).

A case that was brought to the Human Rights and Equal Opportunity Commission of Australia (now called the Australian Human Rights

Commission), and is a clear demonstration of discrimination, concerned the employment arrangements for a woman working in a law firm following the birth of her child. The case highlighted the importance of employers putting in place flexible working arrangements:

Hickie v Hunt & Hunt [1998] HREOCA 8 (9 March 1998)

Marea Hickie, a contract partner with Sydney law firm Hunt & Hunt, brought a complaint against her employer after her request to work part-time following the birth of her child was refused. She claimed the firm had given away her client base while she was on maternity leave. In a complaint heard by HREOCA, Commissioner Evatt found that the law firm had indirectly discriminated against Ms Hickie by requiring her to work full-time in order to maintain her practice. The firm was ordered to pay $95 000 in compensation.

The fundamental differences between bullying and discrimination are the types of behaviours that constitute discrimination:

- they do not have to be repeated, unlike bullying;
- they have to be relevant to particular characteristics of the target, unlike bullying; and
- they have to involve unfair treatment of an individual, which may or may not be the case in bullying.

Box 2.2 Discrimination in my backyard

Information about discrimination and harassment is organised differently in different jurisdictions. In some places, information can be found under 'anti-discrimination' while, in others, under 'equal opportunity'. Similarly, the content of the information can differ. For example, breastfeeding may be specifically listed as a ground for discrimination or it could be subsumed under 'sex'. In the Australian Capital Territory, one's profession, trade, occupation or calling is included as grounds for discrimination or harassment (*Discrimination Act, Australian Capital Territory, 1991*).

Care should be taken to use the criteria relevant to your jurisdiction, and to make sure that all the factors have been considered before claiming harassment or discrimination. For example, most Australian legislation describes situations in which discrimination is unlawful, such as in employment, education, sport, accommodation, selling or transferring land, and providing goods and services (Victorian Equal Opportunity and Human Rights Commission 2008; *New South Wales Anti-discrimination Act 1977*). Some states also have additional legislation that is related to discrimination and harassment. For example, in South Australia, legislation exists to protect whistleblowers from unfair treatment (Equal Opportunity Commission South Australia 2009). Links to all Australian state and territory anti-discrimination/equal opportunity resources can be found www.beyondbullying.com.au.

While there are some differences in legislation, and discrimination and harassment claims are administered by different authorities, it is also important to note that harassment is viewed in the same way internationally. Resources all around the world echo that harassment is behaviour that is unwanted, offensive, humiliating or intimidating according to the reasonable person, and that it is based on one or more grounds for discrimination, such as race, sex or age (see Canadian Human Rights Commission 2004; USA Equal Employment Opportunity Commission 2007; Citizens Information Board of Ireland 2008).

Bullying and harassment

Harassment is usually defined as unsolicited behaviour that offends, humiliates or intimidates, and focuses on some particular characteristic of the targeted individual (Anti-discrimination Board of New South Wales 2005). The characteristics are the same as those listed in anti-discrimination legislation (race, sex, age, disability and so on). As recognised in Box 2.2, international sources converge on this definition of harassment.

Harassment is fundamentally different to bullying because behaviours that constitute harassment:

- do not have to be repeated to be considered harassment, unlike bullying which requires repeated behaviours; and
- have to be on the basis of some characteristic of the target, unlike bullying.

Bullying and violence

Workplace violence is defined as 'any action, incident or behaviour that departs from reasonable conduct in which a person is assaulted, threatened, harmed, or injured in the course of, or as a direct result of, his or her work' (International Labor Organization 2003). Our discussion of violence will be limited to 'worker-on-worker violence'; that is, violence that occurs between employees in an organisation (Mayhew 2004), because it is most relevant to workplace bullying.

Bullying and workplace violence are certainly related. They may both be preceded by conflict (for example, dispute-related bullying, Einarsen 1999); but bullying does not always escalate into violence. There are also some important distinctions, though. As discussed previously, bullying can be quite subtle, and consist of the absence of behaviours (for example, leaving people off email lists). Physical violence is usually more noticeable, both when it is occurring and in its aftermath (for example, visible physical injury). The legal avenues available following workplace violence are also different, because violent acts (such as threats and physical assaults) are covered by criminal law (Barron 2002).

Box 2.3 Case study: Nationwide News Pty Ltd

This case demonstrates how bullying, harassment, discrimination and violence can all occur together. In the case of *Nationwide News Pty Ltd v Naidu; ISS Security Pty Ltd v Naidu (no 2) [2008] NSWCA 71 (24 April 2008)*, a judge of the NSW Court of Appeal found Nationwide News liable for 'a severe form of bullying' perpetrated by one of its employees on a contracted security guard, Mr Devandar Naidu.

Mr Naidu was frequently racially vilified, harassed on the basis of his race, physically and sexually assaulted, and bullied over a four-year period (1992–1996). Evidence was given that Mr Naidu was repeatedly called names, including 'prick', 'monkey face', 'coconut head' and 'poofter'. He was grabbed and pushed, yelled at and threatened with physical violence. Items of furniture were thrown at him. Mr Naidu was made to work excessive, unpaid hours. He was touched in a sexually inappropriate way and was threatened with job loss if he didn't perform work on the perpetrator's private home.

Mr Naidu suffered severe psychological injury. He was awarded around AUD$1.9 million in damages.

Why are the distinctions important?

Bullying, harassment, discrimination, conflict and violence can, of course, occur together at the same time. We hear about such complex cases if they go to court and are highly publicised, or attract attention due to the severity of the behaviours. The distinctions between these issues are not pointed out to downplay the severity of such events, nor to suggest that they can be dissected and easily compartmentalised. In cases where some combination of bullying, harassment, discrimination, conflict and violence do occur together, the distinctions between them may not be so important because there are already established laws and practices for dealing with discrimination, harassment and violence (see Chapter 5 for a brief review of relevant laws). To the extent that these behaviours occur independently of one another, however, strategies specific to each need to be implemented.

One of the practical reasons why these issues need to be disentangled is that they can happen to anyone, regardless of personal characteristics. As discussed, harassment occurs on the basis of some characteristic such as race, sex or marital status. If we focus only on harassment, or make bullying part of harassment, what about the people who are treated poorly at work, who do not possess any of the characteristics listed in the anti-discrimination legislation? A few examples may demonstrate the point more clearly.

On three occasions, Sean has been assigned more work than can be reasonably done by one person before the required deadlines. Subsequently, his immediate boss has yelled at him for not meeting the deadlines, and called him 'useless' in the common area of the office. Sean worked after-hours for two of the last three projects, trying to meet the deadlines. His performance has been rated as satisfactory for the last four years. His workplace has a harassment policy, which he has consulted, but the behaviour he has endured does not meet the criteria. Sean is an Anglo-Saxon male who is not religious. He is married and does not have a disability.

This example demonstrates some problems associated with focusing only on harassment. People who possess none of the characteristics outlined as 'grounds' for harassment can still experience unreasonable behaviours at work. Bullying should have been added to the organisation's policy and procedures in a comprehensive manner, with a clear understanding of how it relates to harassment. We'll talk more about what organisations should do in Chapters 6 and 7. Let's consider a further example:

Angie is an enrolled nurse. In front of other nurses and patients, she has been called names by her Nurse Unit Manager (NUM). The name calling and frequent snide remarks have referred to her hair colour. She is an attractive young woman with blonde hair. Angie has noticed, from talking to other nurses, that none of her requests for time off or requests for shift changes have been approved by the NUM in the last six months. Other nurses are regularly having their shifts changed. Angie is an evangelical Christian, but others who are openly Christian in her workplace are not treated in this way. Angie has often seen her NUM attending Angie's church.

This example demonstrates another danger of only focusing on harassment. There was no evidence that Angie was harassed on the basis of a characteristic that could be 'grounds' for harassment—such as religious beliefs. She was targeted by bullying behaviour. People who do possess characteristics that could be 'grounds' for harassment and discrimination can be treated poorly at work independent of those characteristics. A harassment policy alone does not cover these situations.

Social norms and values

In terms of recognition, workplace bullying is something like the new kid on the block. Harassment and violence have been known problems in the workplace and other contexts for some time. This is not to say that bullying has never happened before—it has, but may have been called something else; for example, 'office politics'. Violence has been socially devalued for a long time, ever since humans started organising themselves in societies. Harassment related to sex, race, religion and so on, has been socially devalued with the advent and growth of the women's liberation movement (see Gomes et al. 2004; Sev'er 1996; Wiener & Gutek 1999). Employers are now quite used to having anti-harassment policies and equal-opportunity employment strategies. Social values have made harassment and violence unacceptable. Bullying has similar negative effects on people, and needs to be similarly devalued by society. One way of doing this is to make bullying part of harassment, but we have already discussed why this is inappropriate. The risk of not recognising bullying as related to but distinct from harassment, violence and conflict is that the unique elements of bullying, which distinguish it from the other issues, will not be catered for. These unique elements include some factors that we have already covered, such as:

- the kinds of behaviours that bullying involves (see Chapter 1);
- the kinds of situations in which bullying can happen (see above);
- the repetitiveness of the behaviours;
- the potential subtlety of the behaviours;
- the issues around reporting and gathering evidence; and
- the role of the organisation and organisational context (see Chapter 4).

If an organisation only has a strategy to deal with harassment, then bullying is dealt with only to the extent to which it overlaps with harassment. The same can be said if an organisation has a strategy in place for dealing with violence: bullying is taken care of to the extent to which it overlaps with violence. Having a risk management strategy for workplace bullying ensures complete and effective management of the unique aspects of bullying when they occur with other issues and when they occur alone.

References

American Psychiatric Association 2000, *Diagnostic and Statistical Manual of Mental Disorders* (4th ed.), Washington: APA.

Anti-discrimination Act of NSW 1977.

Anti-discrimination Board of New South Wales 2005, ADB Factsheet: Discrimination and the Anti-discrimination Board of NSW.

Babiak, P. & Hare, R. 2006, *Snakes in Suits: When psychopaths go to work*, New York: Harper Collins.

Barron, O. 2002, Why workplace bullying and violence are different: Protecting employees from both, in M. Gill, B. Fisher & V. Bowie (Eds.), *Violence at Work: Causes patterns and prevention*, Devon: Willan Publishing.

Canadian Human Rights Commission 2009, Discrimination and harassment, retrieved 5 February 2009, from http://www.chrc-ccdp.ca/discrimination/harassment-en.asp

Caponecchia, C. & Wyatt, A. 2007, The problem with 'workplace psychopaths', *Journal of Occupational Health and Safety Australia and New Zealand, 23*, 403–6.

—— 2008, Victimising the 'bully': The problem with the 'workplace psychopaths' approach, paper presented at the 6th International Conference on Workplace Bullying.

—— 2009, Distinguishing between bullying, harassment and violence: A risk management approach, *Journal of Occupational Health and Safety Australia and New Zealand, 25*(6), 439–49.

Citizens Information Board of Ireland 2008, Harassment and sexual harassment, retrieved 5 February 2009, from http://www.citizensinformation.ie/categories/employment/equality-in-work/harassment_at_work

Clarke, J. 2005, *Working with Monsters: How to identify and protect yourself from the workplace psychopath*, Sydney: Random House.

Condliffe, P. 2008, *Conflict Management* (3rd ed.), Sydney: LexisNexis Butterworths.

Discrimination Act, Australian Capital Territory, 1991.

Einarsen, S. 1999, The nature and causes of bullying, *International Journal of Manpower, 20*, 16–27.

Equal Opportunity Commission South Australia 2009, Victimisation and whistleblowing fact sheet, retrieved 31 March 2010, from http://www.eoc.sa.gov.au/site/home.jsp

Gomes, G.M., Owens, J. & Morgan, J.F. 2004, Prohibiting sexual harassment in the European Union, *Employee Relations, 26*(3), 292–306.

Hadikin, R. & O'Driscoll, M. 2000, *The Bullying Culture: Cause, effect, harm reduction*, Melbourne: Books for Midwives.

Hare, R. 1996, Psychopathy and antisocial personality disorder: A case of diagnostic confusion, *Psychiatric Times, 13*(2), 129–132.

Hill, C. 2006, Bullying and harassment intervention campaign: Bullying exposed. Paper presented at the Compliance, Performance, and Beyond 2006 Comcare OHS conference, Canberra.

Hicklin, J. & Widiger, T.A. 2005, Similarities and difference among antisocial and psychopathic self-report inventories from the perspective of general personality functioning, *European Journal of Personality, 19*, 325–42.

Hockley, C. 2002, *Silent Hell: Workplace violence and bullying*, Norwood: Peacock Publications.

International Labor Organization (ILO) 2003, Code of practice on workplace violence in services sectors and measures to combat this phenomenon, Geneva: International Labor Organization.

Keashly, L. & Nowell, B.L. 2003, Conflict, conflict resolution, and bullying, in S. Einarsen, H. Hoel, D. Zapf & C.L. Cooper (Eds.), *Bullying and Emotional Abuse in the Workplace: International perspectives in research and practice* (1st ed., pp. 339–58), London: Taylor & Francis.

Mayhew, C. 2004, The overlaps between occupational violence/bullying and systemic pressures on organizations from global markets, in P. McCarthy & C. Mayhew (Eds.), *Safeguarding the Organization Against Violence and Bullying*, Houndsmills: Palgrave Macmillan.

Parker, R. 2008, *The management and operations of the ambulance service of NSW*, Sydney: NSW Parliament Legislative Council, General Purpose Committee No. 2.

Sev'er, A. 1996, Mainstream neglect of sexual harassment as a social problem, *Canadian Journal of Sociology, 21*(2), 185–202.

Silkstone, D. 2007, 31 May 2007, Beware the psycho boss: The new enemy within, *The Age*.

South Australian Occupational Health and Safety Act 1986, § 55A.

Stranks, J. 2005, *Stress at Work: Management and prevention*, Oxford: Elsevier.

USA Equal Opportunity Commission 2007, Harassment, retrieved 5 February 2009, from http://www.eeoc.gov/types/harassment.html

Victorian Equal Opportunity and Human Rights Commission 2008, Types of discrimination, retrieved 2 February 2009, from http://www.humanrights commission.vic.gov.au/types%20of%20discrimination/default.asp

Weiner, R.L. & Gutek, B.A. 1999, Advances in sexual harassment research, theory and policy, *Psychology, Public Policy and Law*, 5(3), 507–18.

CHAPTER 3. HOW COMMON IS BULLYING, AND WHAT DOES IT COST?

One of the first steps in trying to prevent and manage workplace bullying is understanding how frequently it occurs. This chapter reviews the data on the prevalence of bullying in the working population, and some of the reasons why it is difficult to know exactly how common bullying is in a particular workplace. Despite variations in prevalence, we know that bullying is very costly for individual targets, organisations, and the community.

How big is the problem?

There are no definitive statistics on the prevalence of workplace bullying, and obtaining reliable data is complicated by several issues. Prevalence figures depend to a large extent on how bullying is measured and defined (see Hoel et al. 1999). Measurement and definition of bullying varies across studies (for example, from using self-reported 'bullying' with supplied definitions of bullying, to using indices of bullying behaviours with different scoring methods, see Salin 2001). There is a lack of widespread national surveillance systems, and we know that people under- and over-report being bullied. Cultural differences in how bullying is viewed, and how it is reported (for example, influenced by legislative frameworks, the role of unions, or social conventions) also affect observed differences in prevalence figures. Accordingly, it is difficult to compare the various figures available from academic or industry research, and across jurisdictions. Rather than go into the detail of how the studies differ, and attempt comparison, we will give an indication of the types of prevalence figures that are available.

Looking across several European studies, severe bullying is thought to be experienced by 1–4 per cent of the working population, while less severe bullying is experienced by 8–10 per cent (Zapf et al. 2003). Norwegian studies have placed the prevalence of bullying at 6 per cent, using different methodologies, although Norway is thought to be different to many other jurisdictions due to cultural and economic factors (Nielsen et al. 2009).

In a national survey of 1518 people by Australian job search website CareerOne in 2007, 74 per cent of respondents said they had been bullied in the workplace at some time and 22 per cent of the survey respondents had 'just quit' their job rather than doing anything else about it (CareerOne 2007). A survey by recruitment firm Drake International of 850 Australian workers indicated that 25 per cent had been bullied in the previous six months (Drake International 2009), while more than 50 per cent said they had witnessed bullying.

Public sector authorities in Australia have started to monitor workplace bullying as part of their regular staff surveys, though bullying and harassment are often confused with one another in these data. The Victorian public sector *People Matter Surveys* of 2006 (over 13 000 responses) and 2007 (just under 16,000 responses) both indicated that 21 per cent of the workforce claimed to have been targeted by 'harassment or bullying behaviours' in the previous twelve months (State Services Authority of Victoria 2006, 2007). It is not clear from these data what proportion of the behaviours would have constituted bullying and what proportion would have constituted harassment. The Tasmanian State Service Employee Survey Report 2005 (nearly 11 000 respondents) revealed that 26 per cent of Tasmanian public-service workers reported being subject to 'harassment or bullying' in the previous twelve months (Tasmanian State Services Commissioner 2005). Forty per cent said they had witnessed bullying and harassment. In the 2006–2007 Tasmanian report, 15 per cent claimed to have been harassed or bullied (Tasmanian State Services Commissioner 2007). Australian federal public service figures place the prevalence at 15 per cent of the workforce being 'bullied' in the last twelve months (Australian Public Service Commission 2007).

In the 2006 Victorian survey, more than 40 per cent of respondents were concerned about reprisals for lodging a grievance (State Services Authority Victoria 2006). This was echoed in the Drake International survey (2009), where only 50 per cent of targets sought assistance. The reasons most frequently cited for not seeking help were the beliefs that nothing would be done, or that reporting the behaviour would make it worse.

Taking these figures together, despite methodological differences, it seems reasonably conservative to conclude that bullying is occurring to about 10 per cent of the working population. This means that one in ten people are experiencing bullying. Even if the real figure was closer to 5 per cent (one in twenty), this would still constitute a very large sector of the workforce. Reliable, valid and comparable data which distinguish between bullying and other unacceptable behaviours still present an important research priority. These data would help make the case that prevention is of utmost importance.

Why don't people report workplace bullying?

As mentioned previously, the available statistics on how often bullying occurs probably underestimate the true incidence of bullying, because people do not always report it. In the health system, nurses have described reporting workplace bullying as 'professional suicide' (Garling 2008, section 12.26). Let's consider some of the other reasons why people don't report workplace bullying.

Subtlety of the behaviours

Some of the behaviours that are considered to be bullying, if they meet the other criteria discussed in Chapter 1, can be enacted with great subtlety. For example, not including someone in an email list (Rayner 2007) could mean that person is unable to adequately prepare for a meeting, and thus their credibility and opportunity to contribute is undermined. Regularly moving or rearranging items in someone's workspace can cause extreme frustration, and interfere with their work performance and progress. These behaviours can be quite hard to detect and to assign responsibility for because they sometimes involve omissions, or occur in secret. If they were reported, these behaviours could be dismissed as forgetfulness, misunderstanding, miscommunication, 'technical problems', or as though nothing at all has happened. Subtle actions such as these may lead the target of the behaviour to question if anything is really happening to them, or wonder if the problems may actually be their own fault. As targets quietly suffer and ask, 'Is it just me?', the behaviour goes unreported.

Embarrassment

Related to the subtlety of the behaviours, people may feel embarrassed about reporting some of the behaviours that are considered to be bullying. The behaviour itself may have caused some personal embarrassment (like a school prank of putting glue on someone's chair), or the act of reporting it to a manager may be embarrassing. Imagine having to report to your supervisor or human relations officer that someone keeps leaving rotten food in your desk drawer. For many people, doing this would be like 'telling the teacher', and the implication that they couldn't handle it themselves could also cause embarrassment and shame. Their perception of the likely response from management, which might include laughter or being told to 'learn to take a joke', may compound this problem.

Fear

In the United Kingdom, 95 per cent of a large sample of public sector trade unionists supported the idea that workers are too scared to report workplace bullying (Rayner 1998, 1999). There are several things that people may fear if they report bullying. Firstly, they may fear that they will lose their job. This is an extremely potent fear, especially in times of economic uncertainty. Alternatively, people may not have a lot of confidence in their superior's attitude to the problem, and fear that they will not be taken seriously. They might think that they will be told to 'toughen up' or 'roll with the punches'. The target may also fear how they will be perceived for having reported bullying—for example, as a troublemaker, or as untrustworthy.

A real fear may exist regarding retribution or 'payback'. If bullying is reported and not dealt with appropriately, the behaviours may continue in a more subtle, covert manner. We know that almost 40 per cent of people who have experienced bullying or harassment are concerned with the negative consequences of making a complaint (State Services Authority of Victoria 2006).

Not knowing what to do

In some situations, targets have no real means for taking action and thus reporting does not occur. Targets may not know what constitutes inappropriate behaviour or to what type of behaviour they have been exposed—for example, bullying as opposed to harassment or just poor/unfair management practices. They may not know what to do should they encounter bullying behaviour because they have not been trained to recognise it, nor been made aware of the internal complaint or grievance procedures. Sometimes there are no procedures in place.

The role of the person using bullying behaviours

In some cases, the position of the person using the bullying behaviours can make bullying more difficult for targets and witnesses to report. Many organisations, understandably, want to resolve any kind of workplace dispute or complaint as locally as possible (see Parker 2008). This means that immediate supervisors often have a role in dealing with complaints of workplace bullying and other unacceptable behaviours.

In addition to all the reasons people don't report workplace bullying, reporting to your immediate supervisor is a particular problem if that supervisor is the person using the unacceptable behaviours. Many organisations recognise this problem and advise targets to report to the next highest supervisor if this is the case. An issue often overlooked, however, is conflicts of interest in the reporting lines. Supervisors can have all sorts of conflicts of interest which make them inappropriate for dealing with workplace bullying claims; for example, the supervisor is best friends with the accused, or married to them, or the accused is their sports coach. Conflicts of interests *must* be engineered out of reporting lines for workplace bullying and other unacceptable behaviours if the reporting process is to be fair. We examine the conflicts of interest issue further in Chapters 6 and 7.

The role of immediate supervisors as the first port of call when reporting workplace bullying also raises the issue of training and experience. Line managers/supervisors are often not trained to deal with unacceptable behaviours. Despite being highly skilled in their jobs, many have little formal management training. The problems of requiring line managers to deal with complex situations involving conflict, bullying and unacceptable behaviours, with little management training, were recognised in the findings of the inquiry into the New South Wales Ambulance Service (see Parker 2008). If line managers and supervisors are expected to be the 'front line' in workplace bullying reporting, then they need training and support for this function. A lack of training in what bullying is and how it should be dealt with can contribute to less than adequate outcomes for targets and for those accused of workplace bullying. While centralised reporting procedures would seem an obvious remedy, these can also have significant problems (for example, in terms of timeliness, confidentiality, and independence), as we discuss in Chapter 7.

If a high performer is the person using bullying behaviours, then the problem can be particularly difficult. This person may be a key player in terms of financial gain for the organisation, or they may be 'protected' because they have special skills or knowledge (Rayner 2007). Organisations sometimes turn a blind eye to unacceptable behaviours in order to retain the individual(s) and the benefits they contribute. The challenge of doing something about bullying can cost the organisation money. In the long run, however, managing it can also significantly save the organisation, increase its performance and staff commitment, and improve its reputation. There are several ways to help avoid individuals becoming so singularly important to the organisation, such as succession planning, training and mentoring, and professional development. These can avoid the difficulties of bullying should it occur, and avoiding dependence on a few individuals makes good business sense.

Nature of the industry

In many cases, factors related to the type of industry or industry sector create barriers to reporting the extent of workplace bullying. For example, bullying is known to be a problem in many hierarchical or paramilitary organisations, which emphasise discipline in order to achieve a particular outcome (for example, Parker 2008; Archer 1999).

When bullying occurs in small business, it may be difficult for the targeted person to do anything about it. In small businesses, often the only people to whom the targeted person can report are either the perpetrator(s) of the bullying behaviour, or someone with some form of conflict of interest (for example, a relative of the alleged perpetrator). This is why it may appear that the only course of action for employees in this situation is to leave their job. This set of circumstances is often compounded if bullying occurs in a small family business and employees are subject to bullying behaviours perpetrated by their own relatives. Family businesses are often under-resourced. Unfortunately, other pressures associated with running a small business can make good health and safety management and consultation with employees about their work experiences less of a management priority.

Some of the reasons for not reporting bullying are a consequence of the behaviours themselves, while others are more within the control of the organisation. Organisations can design comprehensive, independent and confidential reporting systems, they can train people in how to report bullying, and can increase awareness of how subtle behaviours can be used to slowly undermine people. Part of the purpose of this book is to help people and organisations to become more aware of workplace bullying, and to challenge them to develop better systems that circumvent the problems highlighted above. More about what organisations should do regarding reporting the hazard of workplace bullying can be found in Chapter 6.

The costs of workplace bullying

Workplace bullying incurs a great cost to targets and organisations. These costs can be expressed in dollars, time, and pain and suffering, and while it can seem crude to reduce a workplace hazard to a dollar cost, this is sometimes the most effective way of gaining organisational commitment to prevention strategies. Figures from the Australian Productivity Commission (2010) indicate that stress, of which bullying is a part, costs organisations $10.1 billion annually through absenteeism and presenteeism, and costs the economy $14 billion annually. These figures do not include the costs of turnover, retraining, and effects of reduced morale on productivity across the wider work group. While these costs are significant, the problem with large-scale economic models of how much psychological hazards cost is that, due to their scale, they can seem quite remote from everyday business operations. A simple examination of the likely effects of bullying on individual businesses demonstrates how bullying can represent a significant financial cost.

Box 3.1 How much could bullying cost your organisation?

Use the checklist below to start a tally of how much workplace bullying might cost your organisation. You might like to set some assumptions to get more accurate figures (for example, one in ten staff being bullied per year; 40 per cent turnover of those who are bullied per year, etc). Note that many of the costs are not insurable.

Production losses

- overhead costs while production is reduced
- time lost due to preoccupation with the negative situation
- production lost due to absenteeism
- production lost due to presenteeism
- time lost due to internal transfer
- time lost when people look for a new job in work time
- time lost when people prepare their case
- loss of skill and experience when a person leaves
- loss of institutional knowledge when a person leaves
- lowered (at least initial) production rates of replacement workers

Wage losses

- interruption of work due to the negative situation
- person hours spent in 'damage control'
- costs of people taking full leave entitlements
- costs of redundancy payouts
- costs of replacing staff (for example, administration, advertising, selection costs)

Associated costs

- costs related to investigations (internal and/or external) including the gathering of evidence and the preparation of reports
- costs of implementing report recommendations e.g. costs of external advisors to facilitate the recovery of the organisation, development and implementation of appropriate policies and procedures (for example, relating to dispute resolution and disciplinary action)
- costs of supporting other workers such as bystanders (for example, through provision of counselling)
- costs of training new staff
- legal and other costs associated with prosecution and common law claims
- cost of fines imposed by health and safety authorities
- some medical costs (for example, in relation to diagnosis)

Insurance premiums

- increased insurance premiums due to claims experience

Intangibles

- lowered employee commitment and therefore poorer performance
- lowered employee motivation
- lowered employee morale
- loss of reputation as an employer (for example, through poor publicity)
- loss of goodwill
- cost of various forms of retaliation towards the organisation by aggrieved parties

Costs to the individual

The effects of workplace bullying on targets is one area that has received a great deal of research attention. The nature and extent of these costs depends a lot on the nature of the bullying behaviours, how long they go on for, and the nature and efficacy of the processes that are used to deal with them after they occur (for example, procedures followed within the organisation, investigation, compensation and litigation). The costs are also influenced by factors intrinsic to the target—their coping styles and the resources they have around them (such as family and friends), and their perceptions and reactions to the bullying behaviour.

Given these differences between people, the differences in the types of bullying behaviours that people could be exposed to, and the various organisational contexts in which they work, it is nearly impossible to give a definitive list of all the possible outcomes that bullying behaviour could have for a particular target. We are able to talk in general about what is typically found to happen to targets, however. There is a wealth of evidence from around the world indicating that bullying results in significant negative consequences for an individual's health. It's important to remember that health includes wellbeing. The World Health Organization's definition of health (WHO 2006) states that, '*Health is a state of complete physical, mental and social well-being and not merely the absence of disease or infirmity.*'

The inclusiveness of 'health' is important because it highlights that psychological symptoms are important health indicators. People who have been exposed to workplace bullying have been found to experience the following:

- post-traumatic stress disorder symptoms[1]
- depression
- anxiety
- sleep disturbances
- lowered self-esteem
- anger
- chronic fatigue
- suicidal thoughts
- irritability

- feelings of nervousness, insecurity and victimisation
- burnout
- musculoskeletal complaints and muscular tension
- headaches
- nausea
- stomach upset
- social withdrawal

(see review in Einarsen & Mikkelsen 2003; Ashforth 1994; Irish Health and Safety Authority 2001; Namie & Namie 2000; see also Parker 2008). Bullying is appropriately viewed as a stressor—that is, something that causes stress (Rayner 1998; Zapf & Gross 2001; Lewis & Orford 2005). Many of these outcomes are similar to those experienced during or following chronic stress. The repeated and enduring nature of bullying means that significant health problems are more likely to occur following bullying than less frequently experienced workplace stressors (Vartia 2001).

Apart from effects on their health, bullying can result in several other outcomes for targets, including:

- reduced productivity (Ashforth 1994);
- reduced job satisfaction (Einarsen et al. 1998);
- dreading going to work (CareerOne, 2007);
- decreased problem-solving abilities, concentration and rational judgment (Irish Health and Safety Authority 2001);
- reduced self-confidence, self-worth and productivity (Price Spratlen 1995); and
- increased propensity to leave the workplace (Quine 2001), or thoughts of leaving the workplace (State Services Authority of Victoria 2006).

Studies which show that targets of bullying experience particular outcomes are mainly correlational in that they provide information about events that occur together. Just because events occur together does not necessarily mean that one of them has directly, independent of other factors, caused the other. It may have been one of multiple contributing factors. Scientific evidence to suggest causation of negative outcomes by bullying and related issues is growing. A prospective study of 8130 men and 7400 women in

Finland has shown that those experiencing conflicts at work had a greater risk of developing psychiatric conditions four to six years following the conflicts (Romanov et al. 1996). Also, in a study of 4981 female and 674 male nurses in Finland, the 5 per cent of nurses who reported being bullied had a 26 per cent higher risk of sickness absence compared to non-bullied employees (Kivimaki et al. 2000).

The issue of causation is also relevant to the observation that in some cases, bullying has been argued to have led to people taking their own lives and the lives of others. Cases involving suicide and/or homicide tend to be the ones covered in the media, and to some extent they are extreme cases. There is often a debate (legal or otherwise) in such situations regarding the degree to which being bullied 'caused' a person to attempt or complete suicide, or to experience other symptoms mentioned above.

The outcomes that targets experience can be caused by multiple factors combined, and the cumulative effects of stressors are well known (Evans & Coman 1993; McFarlane & Bryant 2007). In leading to a set of outcomes, it is likely that being bullied combines with a host of other experiences including, but not limited to:

- the target's past experiences;
- the nature and extent of their reactions to the situation;
- the other stressors in their job or workplace independent of bullying;
- the nature and efficacy of their coping strategies; and
- other significant events in their lives.

This does not mean that the symptoms experienced after bullying are the target's 'fault', however. We know that bullying generally results in negative outcomes, as listed above, but we are not able to say in a specific case that particular bullying behaviours uniquely and independently caused a particular negative outcome(s). Assessing the extent to which being bullied causes certain outcomes for a particular person needs to be done with all the contextual factors in mind, as well as considering what we know generally happens following workplace bullying. A final assessment comes down to a question of what is reasonable. We need to ask whether it is reasonable to expect that significant negative psychological outcomes are likely to have occured for a particular individual after experiencing particular kinds of workplace bullying, having taken into account individual differences and contextual factors.

References

American Psychiatric Association. 2000, *Diagnostic and Statistical Manual of Mental Disorders* (4th ed.), Washington: APA.

Archer, D. 1999, Exploring 'bullying' culture in the para-military organisation, *International Journal of Manpower, 20*(1/2), 94–105.

Ashforth, B. 1994, Petty tyranny in organisations, *Human Relations, 47*(7), 755–78.

Australian Public Service Commission 2007, State of the Service Report 06–07, Canberra: Australian Public Service Commission.

Australian Productivity Commission 2010, Performance Benchmarking of Australian Business Regulation: Occupational health and safety, Canberra: Australian Government Productivity Commission.

CareerOne 2007, Australian workforce infested with bullies, retrieved 25 July 2007, from http://media.monster.com/CMS/auen/seeker/pdf/CareerOne-Bullies-in-the-workplace.pdf

Drake International 2009, Bullying research report: Drake International Pty Ltd.

Einarsen, S., Matthiesen, S. & Skogstad, A. 1998, Bullying, burnout and well-being among assistant nurses, *Journal of Occupational Health and Safety Australia and New Zealand, 14*(6), 563–8.

Einarsen, S. & Mikkelsen, E.G. 2003, Individual effects of exposure to bullying at work, in S. Einarsen, H. Hoel, D. Zapf & C.L. Cooper (Eds.), *Bullying and Emotional Abuse in the Workplace: International perspectives in research and practice*, (1st ed., pp. 127–144), London: Taylor and Francis.

Evans, B.J. & Coman, G.J. 1993, General versus specific measures of occupational stress: An Australia police survey, *Stress Medicine, 9*, 11–20.

Garling, P. 2008, Final Report of the Special Commission of Inquiry: Acute care services in NSW public hospitals (Vol. 1), Sydney.

Hoel, H., Rayner, C. & Cooper, C.L. 1999, Workplace bullying, in C.L. Cooper & I.T. Robertson (Eds.), *International Review of Industrial and Organizational Psychology* (Vol. 14, pp. 195–230), Chichester: Wiley.

Irish Health and Safety Authority 2001, Dignity at Work: The challenge of workplace bullying, Dublin: Irish Health and Safety Authority.

Kivimaki, M., Elovainio, M. & Vahtera, J. 2000, Workplace bullying and sickness absence in hospital staff, *Occupational and Environmental Medicine*, 57, 656–60.

Lewis, S.E. & Orford, J. 2005, Women's experiences of workplace bullying: Changes in social relationships, *Journal of Community & Applied Social Psychology*, 15, 29–47.

Matthiesen, S.B. & Einarsen, S. 2004, Psychiatric distress and symptoms of PTSD among victims of bullying at work, *British Journal of Guidance & Counselling*, 32(3), 335–56.

McFarlane, A.C. & Bryant, R.A. 2007, Post-traumatic stress disorder in occupational settings: Anticipating and managing risk, *Occupational Medicine*, 57, 404–10.

Namie, G. & Namie, R. 2000, *The Bully at Work: What you can do to stop the hurt and reclaim your dignity on the job*, Naperville: Sourcebooks Inc.

Nielsen, M.B., Skogstad, A., Matthiesen, S.B., Glaso, L., Aasland, M.S., Notelaers, G. et al. 2009, Prevalence of workplace bullying in Norway: Comparisons across time and estimation methods, *European Journal of Work and Organizational Psychology*, 18(1), 81–101.

Parker, R. 2008, *The management and operations of the ambulance service of NSW*, Sydney: NSW Parliament Legislative Council, General Purpose Committee No. 2.

Price Spratlen, L. 1995, Interpersonal conflict which includes mistreatment in a university workplace, *Violence and Victims*, 10(4), 285–97.

Quine, L. 2001, Workplace bullying in nurses, *Journal of Health Psychology*, 6(1), 73–84.

Rayner, C. 1998, Workplace bullying: Do something! *Journal of Occupational Health and Safety Australia and New Zealand*, 14, 581–85.

—— 1999, From research to implementation: Finding leverage for prevention, *International Journal of Manpower*, 20(1/2), 28–38.

—— 2007, Preparing for dignity: Tackling indignity at work, in S.C. Bolton (Ed.), *Dimensions of Dignity at Work*: Butterworth Heinemann.

Romanov, K., Appelberg, K., Honkasalo, M.-L. & Koskenvuo, M. 1996, Recent interpersonal conflict at work and psychiatric morbidity: A prospective study of 15,530 employees aged 24–64, *Journal of Psychosomatic Research*, 40(2), 169–76.

Salin, D. 2001, Prevalence and forms of bullying among business professionals: A comparison of two different strategies for measuring bullying, *European Journal of Work and Organizational Psychology*, 10(4), 425–41.

State Services Authority of Victoria 2007, People Matter Survey 2006: Main findings report, Melbourne: State Government of Victoria State Services Authority.

—— 2008, People Matter Survey 2007: Main findings report, Melbourne: State Government of Victoria State Services Authority.

Tasmanian State Service Commissioner 2007, Tasmanian State Service employee survey report, Hobart: Office of the State Service Commissioner.

—— 2005, Employee Survey report 2005, Hobart: Office of the State Service Commissioner.

Vartia, M. 2001, Consequences of workplace bullying with respect to the well-being of targets and the observers of bullying, *Scandinavian Journal of Work Environment and Health*, 27(1), 63–9.

World Health Organization 2006, Preamble to the constitution of the World Health Organization (45th ed.): World Health Organization.

Zapf, D. & Gross, C. 2001, Conflict escalation and coping with workplace bullying: A replication and extension, *European Journal of Work and Organizational Psychology*, 10(4), 497–522.

Zapf, D., Einarsen, S., Hoel, H. & Vartia, M. 2003, Empirical findings on bullying in the workplace, in S. Einarsen, H. Hoel, D. Zapf & C.L. Cooper (Eds.), *Bullying and Emotional Abuse in the Workplace: International perspectives in research and practice*. (1st ed., pp. 103–126), London: Taylor and Francis.

Case study: Evan, Part 1

The following case study is based on real events. We will follow what happened to Evan in instalments throughout the remainder of the book.

Evan, who is 34, works in the emergency services sector. He recently accepted a position based in a regional area. His wife and family have moved from the city so that Evan could take up this job. Evan's previous role included mentoring younger workers in the city, where he was highly respected, highly skilled and well liked. His boss and co-workers were sorry to see him leave but his new job is a step towards greater responsibility, and living in the country is the fulfilment of a dream, because Evan's wife grew up on a farm.

Evan's first few weeks in the new job were great. He had always loved his job but now he started to feel more connected with the community. Evan's wife and children enjoyed being in the country too—they had started a garden and had lots of new pets, but noticed that Evan was not at home very much. He seemed to often be assigned to night duty and was driving very long distances. When he was home, he was very tired and slept a lot.

There were ten other workers at headquarters, including the manager, Bob. Bob grew up in the local area, knows most of the people in town and has been employed at headquarters for 37 years. The other officers have all been employed for at least three years, and two of them, Bob's son and niece, also grew up locally. The officers have adopted a nickname for Evan: 'Slick', short for 'city slicker'. Evan doesn't mind a joke, and he also makes harmless jokes at the expense of other officers, in good-natured fun. It's an accepted part of the culture, both here and back in the city.

About twelve weeks later, in the tea room at headquarters, Evan is stood over by one of his workmates while being verbally abused. Under the pressure of the situation, Evan broke down.

What happened to make things go so wrong?

CHAPTER 4. WHO IS INVOLVED AND WHY DOES IT HAPPEN?

Understanding the individuals involved in workplace bullying, and the interactions between them and the organisation, is fundamental to making sense of this problem. What is it about the targets of bullying behaviour that makes them targets? Why do people who use bullying behaviours perform in such destructive ways? Why do some types of organisations appear to have major bullying problems? In this chapter, we will consider what we know about targets and about people who use bullying behaviours, and talk about the other roles and factors that contribute to whether bullying occurs.

An important theme that we have already touched on, and will keep returning to in this chapter, is that of the importance of context. Several factors combine to influence the nature, duration and occurrence of bullying. Our consideration of these factors therefore needs to be multidimensional. Some of these factors point towards interventions that can be used to prevent and manage bullying more effectively (see Chapters 6 and 7).

Factors influencing the occurrence of bullying

There are several factors that have been shown to contribute to the occurrence of workplace bullying. These include:

- factors specific to the target and the person who displays bullying behaviour;

- factors specific to the organisation's response to bullying, leadership and organisational culture;
- environmental factors in the workplace (such as work design and stressors); and
- factors external to the organisation, such as wider socio-cultural and financial influences (Einarsen et al. 2003; Salin 2003).

We will examine these factors, beginning with a discussion of the issues around personality.

Factors related to individuals

Conventional wisdom would suggest that a major part of the bullying problem is the personality of the individuals involved. Indeed, events that are in some ways similar to workplace bullying are sometimes known as a 'personality clash'. Some researchers have categorically denied that personality has any role at all in explaining workplace bullying (Leymann 1996). Other perspectives imply that personality is the key variable, as we have seen in our discussion of the 'workplace psychopaths' approach (Field 1996; Clarke 2005; Babiak & Hare 2006). Similar to Zapf and Einarsen (2003), our view is that personality is just one of many factors that should be attended to when explaining workplace bullying behaviour.

A complete review of modern academic views on personality and how it can be studied is beyond the scope of this book. Assuming that personality dimensions were related to bullying behaviour (that is, there is a 'bullying personality profile'), we would probably hypothesise that people who used bullying behaviours at work would score low on agreeableness and high on neuroticism. Little experimental work has been done to assess the nature of this relationship. Other studies on personality profiles of targets have found that targets tend to show psychological disturbance (Matthiesen & Einarsen 2001), but it is possible that this is as a result of being bullied, rather than a pre-existing dimension of their personalities (see also Leymann & Gustafsson 1996).

At some level, personality does have an effect on bullying. Even if person-ality variables cannot yet be shown to reliably explain why some people are targets, or others are 'bullies', personality will affect how people interpret and respond to particular situations (Matthiesen & Einarsen 2001). The relationship between personality and bullying appears to be quite complex, and there is a need for longitudinal studies to determine the nature of these relationships. Given this complexity, and the current progress of research, we are a considerable way from being able to use personality variables to help prevent or manage workplace bullying. In the meantime, there are three main problems associated with focusing *solely* on personality as a key determinant of workplace bullying:

- the potential for blame;
- the issues of self-identity and changing behaviour; and
- the fact that anyone can use bullying behaviours.

Blame and personal responsibility

If bullying was just about personality then either of the two main players (the target and the person using bullying behaviours) could be blamed and shamed. This is inconsistent with the values of occupational health and safety. Their behaviour needs to be seen in the context of the situation. The potential for blame has also been cited as a reason for researchers being reluctant to investigate personality traits in relation to workplace bullying (see Milam et al. 2009).

The 'no blame' approach can be a little difficult for targets of workplace bullying to accept. Being able to say that there is something 'wrong' with the personality of the individual who is responsible for the unacceptable behaviours may be an effective way for targets to cope, but it is not necessarily a fair way of approaching workplace bullying in general. In cases where bullying has been proven, the person(s) accused should face the appropriate consequences. We need to maintain an open mind, however, about the factors that might have resulted in the behaviour. Did the organisational culture encourage and/or permit bullying? Did the organisation structure work tasks in such a way that bullying behaviours were more likely? Was there a past conflict that has not been adequately dealt with? None of these considerations can be made if we adopt, by default, the position that personality is the key explanation for bullying. Some of these issues were also discussed in Chapter 2, when talking about the 'workplace psychopaths' approach.

Self-identity and change

In addition, thinking that bullying is only caused by the personality of the person using bullying behaviour can really disadvantage the target. People sometimes view personality as something that cannot change, or equate personality with identity. This could be a real stumbling block in preventing and managing bullying.

Imagine that we did promote the idea that the most important factor in workplace bullying is the personality of the 'bully'. Viewing personality as self-identity means that people could explain away bullying behaviours, claiming that 'It's part of who I am'. Alternatively, people displaying bullying behaviours could become quite distressed at the suggestion that their 'identity' should change because of how it negatively affects others. The reverse could apply to targets. If we promoted the idea that targets become targets because of some inherent deficiency in their personality that makes them weak and vulnerable, then additional pressure would be placed on them to try to change. The common assumption that personality is of prime importance in explaining workplace bullying thus creates unnecessary barriers to dealing with the problem, because of how 'personality' is often interpreted.[2]

Anyone can do it

The other major consideration that argues against focusing on personality as an explanation of workplace bullying is that anyone (with any personality type) could use bullying behaviour at some time. Look back at the criteria and the list of behaviours that are considered to be bullying presented in Chapter 1. Now, be honest. Any of us are capable of engaging in bullying, right? Similarly, any of us could be a target (Rayner 1999).

Related to this, focusing on personality may lead to all sorts of inappropriate strategies to prevent bullying, such as trying to screen out the 'bullies' before employment. Research on workplace bullying is really not yet at a stage where we could be confident in the outcomes of such an approach.

So, personality is a consideration in bullying, because it describes the typical behaviours that we use in a range of situations. In some specific cases, it may be useful in explaining the behaviours and reactions of those involved, but is less so at the general level (Zapf & Einarsen 2003). Relying too heavily on personality as an explanation for why bullying occurs, or as a pathway to a solution, could make the situation considerably worse. Nonetheless, let's review some of the other issues related to the players involved in the workplace bullying process.

Factors related to the target

Targets of workplace bullying are certainly the most researched aspect of the workplace bullying problem (Rayner 1999). They provide data on the incidence of bullying, on the behaviours that are experienced, and the effects the experience has had on them. There is no simple conclusion when considering aspects of the target that can make bullying more likely to occur. Much of the research that is available on this needs to be interpreted with caution, because attributes of the target are often measured after they become targets, so it is unknown whether their 'traits' lead to bullying or bullying leads to their 'traits' (Rayner & Cooper 2006).

There is a tendency to think that the target has 'brought the behaviour upon themselves', shown some kind of weakness, or that somehow 'they were asking for it' (Zapf & Einarsen 2003). While we are accustomed to not blaming the target in the bullying process (see Rayner 1999 for discussion), we need to remember that instances of bullying are multiply determined. To not allow for a role for factors specific to the target would be incomplete (Milam et al. 2009). The exact nature of this involvement would of course need to be determined on a case-by-case basis.

There is some evidence to support the idea that targets can lack social skills, conflict management skills and be unassertive (see Zapf & Einarsen 2003 for review). Targets have been found to have low self-esteem and low social competency, although this was assessed after bullying had occurred (Matthiesen & Einarsen 2007). Other evidence suggests that targets can be 'overachievers' in the workplace. They have been found to be punctual, honest, and rule-bound compared to non-targets (Coyne et al. 2000). These attributes may violate the norms of their workplace, resulting in aggression and undermining behaviour by others (Zapf & Einarsen 2003). Some targets are very capable, professional and accomplished in their job, and envy is thought to be one of the major reasons for workplace bullying (Irish Health and Safety Authority 2001).

The person(s) using bullying behaviours

Little is known about the people who use bullying behaviours in the workplace, and this has sometimes been referred to as the 'black hole' in this research field (Rayner & Cooper 2003). People who display bullying behaviours are a difficult group to access because finding volunteers who admit to having 'bullied' others is quite a challenge (Rayner 1999). Thus, most of what we know about people using bullying behaviours is gleaned from the perspective of the target. Although a major shortcoming in international research, some attempts to study this group are being made (for example, Jenkins et al. 2010).

Males appear to be more likely to be accused of using bullying behaviours than females (Zapf et al. 2003), though this may reflect a reporting bias. While there is evidence to suggest that bullying occurs from someone superior to someone subordinate, bullying is known to frequently occur between peers and from people at a lower level of the organisation to someone at a higher level (Branch et al. 2007).

There have been many attempts to fit bullies into a typology. Some categorisations focus on bullying behaviours and are used to assess whether one type of bullying behaviour, such as malicious gossiping, is more or less prevalent than another (for example, Zapf et al. 2003). Other categorisations, by contrast, seem to focus on the person, suggesting that particular 'types' of bullies have favoured modes of operation (for example, the 'competitive' bully; the self-absorbed bully, the thrill-seeking power hungry bully, Spindel 2008; Kohut 2008; the 'crude' bully, the 'echo' bully, the 'ghost' bully etc., Mueller 2006). These categorisations may be useful for raising awareness but are incomplete and potentially dangerous. They imply that the behaviour is intentional and organised, and that individuals use only one type of bullying behaviour. Paradoxically, though seemingly focused on behaviours, they tend to stigmatise the person through labelling. The labels themselves are based on observation and not always validated by research.

The role of the bystander

There is little research on how the bystander, or observer, of workplace bullying can influence its occurrence, but it is reasonable to assume that through their intervention, workplace bullying situations could be stopped from escalating, or be reported and acted upon. Figures from recruitment firm Drake International suggest that 56 per cent of Australian workers surveyed had witnessed workplace bullying in the last twelve months (Drake International 2009). It is likely that bystanders avoid reporting bullying for some of the same reasons as targets fail to report (such as fear of retribution and not wanting to become involved; see Chapter 3). Bystanders also serve an important role as witnesses to bullying behaviour, and can be asked to corroborate a target's report of workplace bullying or temper over-exaggeration.

Importantly, the relationship between bystanders and the organisation can be negatively affected by witnessing bullying. Bystanders have been found to rate their work environments more negatively than non-observers of workplace bullying (Einarsen et al. 1994). Similar to targets, bystanders report lower job satisfaction and higher levels of job stressors than those not exposed to workplace bullying (Hague et al. 2007; Rayner 1999).

Factors related to the organisation

The organisation's acts and omissions, both before and after bullying occurs, has a significant impact on whether and how bullying manifests. Developing and implementing policy on workplace bullying, or codes of conduct, are obvious examples of how organisations can indicate that bullying behaviours are not acceptable. But just having a policy or code is not enough. So called 'zero-tolerance' policies are often just rhetoric (Caponecchia & Wyatt 2007) because they are not always backed up with a set of actions—reporting procedures, regular system reviews, training and support—and they may not be implemented fairly and consistently. Policies and procedures need to be clear and accessible, and all staff need to be trained in them. Commitment to preventing and managing the problem appropriately must be demonstrated, not just communicated. We will discuss policies and their implementation, as well as other types of interventions, in more detail in Chapters 6 and 7.

The consequences that organisations provide when bullying has occurred also serve as deterrents to the behaviour. Salin (2009) reviews the responses organisations can take, from transferring targets and/or perpetrators, to reconciliatory measures, to punishment, such as demotion and dismissal.

Culture

Apart from overt responses to the workplace bullying problem, organisations can encourage or discourage bullying in an implicit manner by their culture. Organisational culture is commonly referred to as 'the way we do things around here' (Deal & Kennedy 1982). Schein (2004) talks about organisational culture as the shared norms, values and assumptions that are held unconsciously but define how the organisation views itself and its environment. The nature of the culture is identified by observable practices, which have values and underlying assumptions associated with them (see Wilson 2004).

Aspects of organisational culture can affect bullying in several ways. For example, cultural values and practices may 'permit' or encourage acts of bullying, prevent a target from reporting the behaviour (because reporting is seen as weakness) or expect that they will endure it, or make it acceptable for management to ignore reports. Some of the assumptions that may underlie these values include that:

- aggressiveness and bullying behaviours are necessary to get the job done (for example, see Matthiesen et al. 2008 regarding assumptions about bullying in commercial kitchens);
- bullying behaviours 'toughen people up' for the rigours of the industry; and
- bullying behaviours make people know their place in the hierarchy, and some levels of the hierarchy are more important than others.

An example of this might be where junior staff are expected to 'earn their stripes' by taking on large workloads or difficult or undesirable tasks in order to progress through the profession or organisation. Earning one's stripes can be beneficial in developing skills that are not taught in formal professional training. But these experiences may be accompanied by behaviours that are unacceptable, such as public criticism or humiliation that are disguised as 'rites of passage'. Such treatment can become embedded in the way the organisation works, year after year, appointment after appointment. Perpetuating such treatment serves as reinforcement of having ascended the hierarchy and, as such, is difficult to change without serious commitment to cultural change.

The demonstrated values of the organisation are fundamental in preventing and managing workplace bullying. The development of a culture where reports of unacceptable behaviour are taken seriously, dealt with confidentially, fairly and in a timely manner is intrinsic to eradicating workplace bullying and all its negative consequences.

The work environment: job stressors

We have talked about how bullying is considered to be a cause of stress (Rayner 1998; Lewis & Orford 2005), but we also know that bullying is more likely to occur in stressful work environments. While there are several ways of categorising stressors, stressors that relate to the way in which work is designed and organised have often been studied in relation to workplace bullying. These issues can be controlled by the organisation, but rather than being specific to bullying, relate more generally to the system by which the organisation asks employees to fulfil their duties.

Several job stressors have been shown to be related to the occurrence of workplace bullying, including:

- workload and excessive task demands;
- role conflict (the perception that competing demands and expectations are required to fulfil one's job);
- role ambiguity (being unsure about what tasks are part of one's own job, as opposed to someone else's job);
- job insecurity and change;
- unreasonable or negative task-related feedback;

- lack of control over work tasks; and
- lack of social support from co-workers and supervisors

(see Hague et al. 2007; Notelaers, et al. 2009; Matthiesen & Einarsen 2001).

In a representative study in Norway, Hague et al. (2007) found job stressors, including role conflict and interpersonal conflict, together with leadership behaviour, to be the most important predictors of the occurrence of workplace bullying. The study also found that passive leadership or 'laissez-faire' leadership (leaders who avoid making decisions, fail to intervene in conflicts, fail to give feedback and so on) is related to workplace bullying, as is 'destructive leadership', such as tyrannical behaviour (see also Einarsen et al. 2007).

Role conflict and role ambiguity appear to be especially important in predicting cases of workplace bullying (Einarsen et al. 1994; Notelaers et al. 2009). The importance of role conflict and role ambiguity might be explained by attribution theory: conflicting demands and ambiguous roles can be more easily attributed to other people's actions compared to other stressful job characteristics (Notelaers et al. 2009).

The way in which particular stressors influence bullying may well be different in different industries. For example, in organisations where people work in small teams, levels of social support from co-workers may be more important in preventing or enabling bullying compared to poor leadership from senior management, due to the fact that staff spend most time with their colleagues. The relative contribution of particular stressors to the incidence of bullying in a particular workplace can be assessed by local surveys or focus groups. Indeed, measurement of these stressors—and appropriate control strategies—will already occur as part of normal risk management procedures (see Chapter 6). Attempting to control some of these stressors is relatively easy, and is consistent with good management practice. For example, delineating duties in position descriptions can help reduce role ambiguity; distributing work tasks to teams more appropriately can help reduce role conflict; and ongoing professional development, management training, and team building can help improve supervisory relationships and social support at work.

Job content and job context stressors

The knowledge that bullying can occur as a consequence of stressful work conditions can lead some to question the legitimacy of bullying claims. Certain occupations are widely recognised as inherently stressful because of the kinds of tasks that employees are required to undertake. This includes paramedics, emergency services personnel, police and prison officers, military personnel, nurses and other medical staff, due to their potential exposure to traumatic, life-threatening events, coupled with long hours and (often) poor working conditions. Bullying claims in these kinds of jobs are sometimes refuted on the basis that they represent maladjustments to the 'rough and tumble' of these jobs. In other words, stress is expected in the job, and it's the individual's fault if they can't cope.

The evidence suggests, however, that sources of stress in these kinds of jobs are not restricted to the blood, guts and gore. In the case of police work, organisational aspects of the job—that is, relationships with supervisors, work policies, organisational support—have been consistently shown to be as stressful, if not more so, as issues relating to the situations police have to deal with, such as deaths, violence and injuries (Newman & Rucker-Reed 2004; Evans & Coman 1993; Morash et al. 2008; Barron 2008). In many ways these findings make sense because police are specifically trained to deal with life-threatening situations, and this training is likely reinforced through experience.

The distinction between these stressors is sometimes referred to as the 'job-content' versus 'job-context' distinction (Evans & Coman 1993). It is the combination of job-context (supervision, relationships, support etc.) and job-content stressors (exposure to challenging or traumatic situations) that is thought to be what makes police work so demanding. This is supported by information gathered as part of an inquiry into the New South Wales Ambulance Service. When considering the issue of suicides following workplace bullying in the ambulance service, the Legislative Council General Purpose Standing Committee No. 2 heard evidence that: *'suicides and attempted suicides within the Service are a result of bullying and harassment and a lack of support from management, rather than because of what paramedics "see on the road"'* (Parker 2008, p. 22).

The suggestion that bullying symptoms merely represent bad reactions to 'normal' stressful job conditions is common in many situations. This parallels the old saying, 'if you can't stand the heat, get out of the kitchen'. In reality, the kitchen doesn't need to be so hot. Recognising the role of job-context factors is important because these features can often be fixed by organisations, by improving general managerial procedures, the organisation of work tasks, the quality of supervision, feedback, training and professional development. A systematic approach to large scale change such as this will take time and effort, but will pay dividends to all aspects of the organisation's operations.

Box 4.1 Organisational bullying

Some studies document that bullying can be considered to consist of the organisation's practices, rather than the repeated unreasonable behaviour of individuals. While most of our discussion has been about 'interpersonal' bullying, it would be naïve to think that this was the only form of bullying that occurs. Liefooghe and Mackenzie-Davey (2001) investigated the ways in which employees view the term 'bullying', as distinct from academics and administrators. Their research involved conducting focus groups in a telecommunications company in the United Kingdom. Work practices that were considered by employees to constitute bullying included:

- withholding overtime if strict performance goals were not met;
- the use of statistics to monitor performance (sometimes providing a good service to clients conflicted with meeting targets, which exemplified role conflict);
- the use of sickness policy to intimidate staff; and
- threats of discipline, dismissal, or replacement if goals or other operational demands were not met.

These practices, hardwired into the organisational system, had various negative effects on employees, similar to those associated with repeated unreasonable behaviours, such as reduced self-esteem, not wanting to come to work, and feelings of worthlessness, being untrusted and surveilled.

Organisational bullying can trickle down to interpersonal bullying. It was recognised in Liefooghe and Mackenzie-Davey's study that managers were required by the organisation to administer tough expectations, and to discipline staff in order to achieve particular outcomes. In short, they were required to enforce the organisation's practices outlined above. Managers did not want to enforce these expectations and policies, but had little choice. They may have appeared to be bullying their teams, but were following the expectations of their employer. This is like a Nuremberg defence, and indeed, the defence of officers accused of torture in Abu Ghraib prison (see Zimbardo 2007), but demonstrates the importance of not simply demonising people who use bullying behaviours. It may not be the whole story.

The concept of organisational bullying highlights that organisations need to structure their tasks and expectations carefully. Solving organisational bullying goes to the heart of how organisations structure their values into their business plan, and it is not an easy undertaking in a competitive market. At the end of the day, unhappy staff cost money. Achieving a balance between best outcomes for the organisation, and for staff, requires some creative thinking in relation to work design, performance targets and motivation. Preventing and managing workplace bullying, at interpersonal and organisational levels, has to be incorporated into the overall fabric of the organisation to achieve real success.

Socio-cultural factors that may affect bullying

Socio-cultural factors are those outside the organisational sphere which might affect the individuals or the organisation and increase or decrease the likelihood of bullying. These factors could include things such as the economy and social and political factors.

Economic conditions—such as the need to downsize or restructure—can affect the likelihood of workplace bullying. These processes can create a great deal of stress because they decrease job security, thus increasing competition, workloads and potentially resulting in bullying behaviours to 'get the job done' (for example, Hoel & Salin 2003; Salin 2003). People may also be less likely to report workplace bullying at these times for fear of losing their job; and managers may be less likely to notice what is happening because other issues are a higher priority.

There has recently been more focus on how various countries approach workplace bullying differently, as a result of their socio-political history. Some countries and jurisdictions have differing arrangements and relationships with unions, legal frameworks and health and safety practices. These can result in variations in how organisations respond to the problem of workplace bullying, such as whether they see it as their responsibility or not. Similar arguments could be made when comparing particular industries, some of which have very active and vocal union movements. Wider cultural differences have also been suggested as factors that may impact on whether workplace bullying is reported, including individualism versus collectivism, active versus passive cultures, achievement orientation and so on (see Harvey et al. 2009).

The bullying drama spiral

When considering who is involved in workplace bullying, it is important to recognise that bullying is not generally as simple as 'X bullies Y'. What generally happens, over time, is an escalating drama spiral with a number of players, or stakeholders, in varying roles playing out the 'story'. The roles may include 'bully', 'target', 'bystander', people responsible for intervening, family and friends of the various stakeholders, other people who work in the organisation, and possibly the organisation's consumers.

Because there is a lot of under-reporting, the situation may go on unchecked for a period of time over which it typically escalates. The 'drama' attracts more players as time goes by and the situation will reach out and affect other stakeholders. Over time, the original issue may well be lost sight of and the truth radically distorted. People may take and even change sides more than once during the playing out of the drama. Complaints about the bullying behaviours may attract retribution or payback as the momentum of the situation grows. Often the situation will continue until a significant dynamic changes, such as by a person or persons leaving the drama for whatever reason. An example of a case of workplace bullying escalating to involve many players is given in the Appendix.

Workplace bullying generally does not go away. Mostly, the longer it is left, the worse and more complicated the situation gets. The potential for bullying to escalate highlights the importance of using the multiple points of intervention that are available at the individual, organisational and societal levels.

What motivates bullying behaviour?

In the context of these contributing factors, several hypotheses exist to explain why individuals might use bullying behaviour. These motivations are not always mutually exclusive, and instances of bullying may have multiple origins. These factors are mostly hypothesised because, as previously mentioned, individuals who use bullying behaviour are not the easiest group of people with whom to conduct research, simply because most people would not admit to the behaviours. Accordingly, these hypotheses are based on what we know about human behaviour, and on the experiences that targets are able to tell us about. The motivations include (but are not limited to):

- competitiveness—competition for resources (promotion, jobs, money, esteem); where the person sees the target as a threat and therefore seeks to undermine them.
- compensation for deficiency—where a person feels unskilled or deficient in some way, and projects their sense of anxiety, guilt or shame about this deficiency onto someone else as a defence mechanism.
- protection of self-esteem—contrary to conventional wisdom, Baumeister et al. (1996) suggest that high self-esteem, rather than low self-esteem, is a potential motivation for bullying, through its association with aggression. People with high self-esteem may respond aggressively when their high (but unstable) self-esteem is challenged, particularly if their high self-esteem is dependent on validation from others (Zapf & Einarsen 2003; Matthiesen & Einarsen 2007).
- envy—the target has some special skills or resources that the person using bullying behaviours, consciously or unconsciously, covets or wishes to possess (Irish Health and Safety Authority 2001; Adams 1992).

- predatory bullying—the person using the bullying behaviours has singled out a target, perhaps for a reason, or perhaps for no apparent reason (Einarsen 1999). The target may just be an accidental victim, while the person using the bullying behaviours displays power or exploits a weakness (Einarsen et al. 2003).
- dispute-related bullying—a previous conflict or dispute motivates ongoing bullying behaviour (Einarsen et al. 2003; Einarsen 1999).
- performance appraisal or reward structures may unwittingly reward the undermining of others (Salin 2003).
- in-group/out-group dynamics—aspects of social identity theory essentially propose that people are motivated to look after and value their in-group because it enhances their own self-esteem (see Haslam 2004). By contrast, the out-group is devalued, stereotyped and poorly treated. Targets might fall into the 'out-group' of a workplace by appearing different, or occupying an outsider role in some other way. This may especially apply in instances of mobbing, where a group of individuals target an individual (see Box 1.1 in Chapter 1).
- lack of awareness—people using bullying behaviour may be unaware of their behaviour and how it affects others (Richards & Daley 2003). This could be related to a lack of social competence or inability to see things from another's perspective (Zapf & Einarsen 2003; Matthiesen & Einarsen 2007).
- management philosophy—some people using bullying behaviours may think that those behaviours are the only way to ensure the job gets done. They may have been treated in similar ways themselves, and feel that 'running a tight ship' is the only way to get the 'best' out of employees (Crawshaw 2007). These kinds of perspectives can become acculturated in an organisation or industry, similar to the idea that junior staff need to be tested and 'earn their stripes'. Bullying may also result from modelling the behaviour of others in the organisation, or in one's work experience, who have used bullying behaviours.
- workplace change—bullying can be motivated by the desire to remove particular staff from the workplace when dismissing them by normal methods could be difficult or costly (Salin 2003).

Having some information about why people might use bullying behaviours is very important, because it can help targets cope with the situation they are experiencing. It is often quite difficult, however, to know the exact motivation(s) of people using bullying behaviours in specific cases. The above list is intended to give some information on the kinds of motivations that could explain bullying. They may help targets to understand the behaviour a little more; help organisations identify problem issues that may increase the likelihood of bullying (such as a lack of key resources); and help others to reflect on reasons for their behaviour.

References

Adams, A. 1992, *Bullying at Work: How to confront and overcome it*, London: Virago.

Babiak, P. & Hare, R. 2006, *Snakes in Suits: When psychopaths go to work*, New York: Harper Collins.

Barron, S. 2008, Occupational stress: The emerging threat to police officers, *Journal of Occupational Health and Safety Australia and New Zealand, 24*, 553–61.

Baumeister, R.F., Smart, L. & Boden, J.M. 1996, Relation of threatened egotism to violence and aggression: The dark side of high self-esteem, *Psychological Review, 103*, 5–33.

Branch, S., Ramsay, S. & Barker, M. 2007, Managers in the firing line: Contributing factors to workplace bullying by staff—an interview study, *Journal of Management and Organisation, 13*, 264–81.

Caponecchia, C. & Wyatt, A. 2007, The problem with 'workplace psychopaths', *Journal of Occupational Health and Safety Australia and New Zealand, 23*, 403–6.

Clarke, J. 2005, *Working with monsters: How to identify and protect yourself from the workplace psychopath*, Sydney: Random House.

Coyne, I., Seigne, E. & Randall, P. 2000, Predicting workplace victim status from personality, *European Journal of Work and Organizational Psychology, 9*, 335–49.

Crawshaw, L. 2007, *Taming the Abrasive Manager: How to end unnecessary roughness in the workplace*, San Francisco: Jossey-Bass.

Deal, T.E. & Kennedy, A.A. 1982, *Corporate Cultures: The rites and rituals of corporate life*, Reading: Addison Wesley.

Drake International 2009, Bullying research report: Drake International Pty Ltd.

Einarsen, S. 1999, The nature and causes of bullying, *International Journal of Manpower, 20*, 16–27.

Einarsen, S., Hoel, H., Zapf, D. & Cooper, C.L. 2003, The concept of bullying at work: The European tradition, in S. Einarsen, H. Hoel, D. Zapf & C.L. Cooper (Eds.), *Bullying and Emotional Abuse in the Workplace: International perspectives in research and practice* (1st ed., pp. 3–30), London: Taylor & Francis.

Einarsen, S., Raknes, B.I. & Matthiesen, S.B. 1994, Bullying and harassment at work and their relationships to work environment quality: An exploratory study, *European Work and Organizational Psychologist, 4*(4), 381–401.

Einarsen, S., Schanke Aasland, M. & Skogstad, A. 2007, Destructive leadership behaviour: A definition and conceptual model, *The Leadership Quarterly, 18*, 207–16.

Evans, B.J. & Coman, G.J. 1993, General versus specific measures of occupational stress: An Australian police survey, *Stress Medicine, 9*, 11–20.

Field, T. 1996, *Bully in Sight: How to predict, resist, challenge and combat workplace bullying*, Oxfordshire: Success Unlimited.

Harvey, M., Treadway, D., Thompson Heames, J., & Duke, A. 2009, Bullying in the 21st century global organisations:An ethical perspective. *Journal of Business Ethics*, 85, 27–40.

Haslam, S.A. 2004. *Psychology in Organisations: The social identity approach*, London: Sage Ltd.

Hague, L.J., Skogstad, A. & Einarsen, S. 2007, Relationships between stressful work environments and bullying: Results of a large representative study, *Work & Stress, 21*(3), 220–42.

Hoel, H. & Salin, D. 2003, Organisational antecedents of workplace bullying, in S. Einarsen, H. Hoel, D. Zapf & C.L. Cooper (Eds.), *Bullying and Emotional Abuse in the Workplace: International perspectives in research and practice* (1st ed., pp. 203–18), London: Taylor and Francis.

Irish Health and Safety Authority 2001, Dignity at Work: The challenge of workplace bullying, Dublin: Irish Health and Safety Authority.

Jenkins, M., Zapf, D., Winefield, H. & Sarris, A. 2010, *Listening to the bullies: An exploratory study of managers accused of workplace bullying*. Paper presented at the 7th International Conference on Workplace Bullying and Harassment, June 2010, Cardiff, Wales.

Kohut, M.R. 2008, *The Complete Guide to Understanding, Controlling, and Stopping Bullies and Bullying at Work*, Ocala, Florida: Atlantic Publishing Group.

Lewis, S.E. & Orford, J. 2005, Women's experiences of workplace bullying: Changes in social relationships, *Journal of Community & Applied Social Psychology, 15*, 29–47.

Leymann, H. 1996, The Content and development of mobbing at work, *European Journal of Work and Organizational Psychology, 5*(2), 165–84.

Leymann, H. & Gustafsson, A. 1996, Mobbing at work and the development of post-traumatic stress disorders, *European Journal of Work and Organizational Psychology, 5*(2), 251–75.

Liefooghe, A.P.D. & Mackenzie-Davey, K. 2001, Accounts of workplace bullying: The role of the organization, *European Journal of Work and Organizational Psychology, 10*(4), 375–92.

Matthiesen, G.E., Einarsen, S. & Mykletun, R. 2008, The occurrences and correlates of bullying and harassment in the restaurant sector, *Scandinavian Journal of Psychology, 49*, 59–68.

Matthiesen, S.B. & Einarsen, S. 2001, MMPI–2 configurations among victims of bullying at work, *European Journal of Work and Organizational Psychology, 10*(4), 467–84.

—— 2007, Perpetrators and targets of bullying at work: Role stress and individual differences, *Violence and Victims, 22*(6), 735–53.

Milam, A.C., Spitzmueller, C. & Penney, L.M. 2009, Integrating individual differences among targets or workplace incivility, *Journal of Occupational Health Psychology, 14*(1), 58–69.

Morash, M., Kwak, D., Hoffman, V., Lee, C., Cho, S. & Moon, B. 2008, Stressors, coping resources and strategies, and police stress in South Korea, *Journal of Criminal Justice, 36*, 231–9.

Mueller, R. 2006, *Bullying bosses: A survivor's guide. How to transcend the illusion of the interpersonal*: bullyingbosses.com.

Newman, D.W. & Rucker-Reed, M.L. 2004, Police stress, state-trait anxiety, and stressors among U.S. Marshals, *Journal of Criminal Justice, 32*, 631–41.

Notelaers, G., De Witte, H. & Einarsen, S. 2009, A job characteristics approach to explain workplace bullying, *European Journal of Work and Organizational Psychology, 19*(4), 487–504.

Parker, R. 2008, *The management and operations of the ambulance service of NSW*, Sydney: NSW Parliament Legislative Council, General Purpose Committee No. 2.

Rayner, C. 1998, Workplace bullying: Do something! *Journal of Occupational Health and Safety Australia and New Zealand*, 14, 581–5.

—— 1999, From research to implementation: Finding leverage for prevention, *International Journal of Manpower*, 20(1/2), 28–38.

Rayner, C. & Cooper, C.L. 2003, The black hole in 'bullying at work' research, *International Journal of Decision Making*, 4(1), 47–64.

—— 2006, Workplace bullying, in E.K. Kelloway, J. Barling & J.J. Hurrell Jr. (Eds.), *Handbook of Workplace Violence* (pp. 121–46), California, USA: Sage Publications Inc.

Richards, J. & Daley, H. 2003, Bullying policy: Development, implementation and monitoring, in S. Einarsen, H. Hoel, D. Zapf & C.L. Cooper (Eds.), *Bullying and Emotional Abuse in the Workplace: International perspectives in research and practice* (1st ed., pp. 247–58), London: Taylor & Francis.

Salin, D. 2003, Ways of explaining workplace bullying: A review of enabling, motivating and precipitating structures and processes in the work environment, *Human Relations*, 56(10), 1213–32.

Salin, D. 2009, Organisational responses to workplace harassment: An exploratory study, *Personnel Review*, 38(1), 26–44.

Schein, E. 2004, *Organisational culture and leadership* (3rd ed.) Hoboken: John Wiley & Sons.

Spindel, P. 2008, *Psychological Warfare at Work*, Toronto, Ontario, Canada: Spindel & Associates.

Wilson, F.M. 2004, *Organisational Behaviour and Work*, New York: Oxford University Press.

Zapf, D. & Einarsen, S. 2003, Individual antecedents of bullying: Victims and perpetrators, in S. Einarsen, H. Hoel, D. Zapf & C.L. Cooper (Eds.), *Bullying and Emotional Abuse in the Workplace: International perspectives in research and practice* (1st ed., pp. 165–84), London: Taylor & Francis.

Zapf, D., Einarsen, S., Hoel, H. & Vartia, M. 2003, Empirical findings on bullying in the workplace, in S. Einarsen, H. Hoel, D. Zapf & C.L. Cooper (Eds.), *Bullying and emotional abuse in the workplace: International perspectives in research and practice* (1st ed., pp. 103–26), London: Taylor and Francis.

Zimbardo, P. 2007, *The Lucifer effect: How good people turn evil*, London: Rider Books.

part two

RIGHTS AND RESPONSIBILITIES

Case study: Evan, Part 2

About six weeks after arriving, having done a lot of night work, Evan decided to check all the shift rosters in the tea room. As he expected, he had been rostered on night shifts and long-distance jobs at a much higher rate than most other officers. Of the twelve scheduled long trips in the past three weeks, Evan was assigned ten of them. The overtime was good because of the extra money but he was extremely tired, and had hardly spent any time with his family in their new home. It seemed that the normal rules for shift assignment that Evan was used to in the city were not being applied, because Evan had been assigned a majority of night work. He remembered checking rostering patterns with Bob, the station manager, when he was first considering moving to the country. The roster patterns that he saw were the same as the city, consistent with state policy.

Evan decided to talk about this to Bob. He felt it was unfair that he had been assigned all the long trips and night shifts, when others had not. It did not feel like 'sharing the load'. Bob told him that long shifts and long drives were just part of working in the country, because the country is more remote. 'Not everything they do in the city works out here,' said

Bob. Evan expected to have to drive longer distances, but didn't understand why it seemed to be happening mostly to him. Bob told him that he was paranoid.

The long drives and night shifts continued over the next two weeks. Evan was increasingly tired and started being snappy at home. He had tried to get some sleep while at headquarters during night shifts, but the rooms were hot, filled with light, and not comfortable for sleeping.

Evan also noticed that some of the other workers, particularly Amanda, had started to respond to him differently. Amanda, who was responsible for rostering, appeared to avoid him, communicated with him less in the tea room or left the room when he entered. Others refused to swap some shifts with him, but happily swapped with one another. Evan talked to Bob again about the shift assignment, but Bob insisted that long shifts were part of the job. He stated that it was about resourcing, and he blamed the administrators in the city for not giving him more staff. Evan again tried to explain that the shifts appeared to be disproportionately assigned, but he didn't get anywhere with Bob. He raised the issue at the health and safety committee meeting. The chairperson of the committee was Bob's son, Mark. Mark commented, 'Everyone else here had to do their fair share of night shifts and long drives—maybe it's just your turn, Slick.' None of the other officers said anything in response to Evan's complaints. Nothing was done about the shift assignment.

Evan's signs and symptoms of stress and frustration were increasingly showing at home and at work. He was experiencing headaches and a sore jaw from grinding his teeth almost every day, and was relying on pain killers to get through. He informed Bob about these symptoms, and had taken five sick days in the last month. Other workers had noticed that he was looking tired and was being short tempered, which led to further avoidance. Evan dreaded going to work and wondered what would happen next.

CHAPTER 5. THE LEGAL CONTEXT

Knowing where you stand legally is an important consideration for individuals targeted by bullying and organisations faced with the challenge of providing a safe workplace. While it is not our aim to extensively review the law relating to workplace bullying, we refer readers to the sources we have cited for more detail. We will present some major issues in relation to workplace bullying law, describe recent international moves towards law reform, and address the constraints on this process. The existing, relevant law in various countries will be outlined.

Challenges for anti-bullying regulators and international law reform

As awareness increases about workplace bullying and the risk it represents, consideration is being given to the law in this area. Yamada (2003) lists the following purposes for law in relation to workplace bullying:

- encouragement of the prevention of workplace bullying;
- protection of workers and employers who respond promptly, fairly and effectively when informed about bullying behaviour;
- provision of relief for targets of severe workplace bullying, including compensatory damages and reinstatement (if sought); and
- punishment for perpetrators of workplace bullying and their employers.

There are international moves towards law reform in relation to workplace bullying but, as Hoel and Einarsen (2009) explain, there are a number of constraints to overcome in relation to developing appropriate laws. They relate to both legislative frameworks and implementation of laws and include:

- challenges associated with the impreciseness of regulating for intangible and 'shameful' issues (such as workplace bullying);
- lack of involvement/shortcomings in the response of key parties, such as employers, trade unions and the labour inspectorate;
- lack of knowledge, training and education among the key parties;
- fears—especially on the part of employers—that the numbers of reports of workplace bullying will increase with the introduction of such laws;
- difficulties associated with controlling and managing workplace bullying;
- lack of development of an intervention methodology;
- challenges related to economic downturns; and
- withdrawal of state support to occupational health services.

Nevertheless, there have been many workplace bullying cases successfully litigated in many countries which 'demonstrates that the regulatory avenue is not closed' (Hoel & Einarsen 2009). Clearly, any laws pertaining to workplace bullying must embrace a multi-pronged preventive approach and be well understood by those required to implement and administer them.

International examples of law in relation to workplace bullying

Australia

In Australia, workplace bullying behaviour is considered to be a health and safety hazard because it has the potential to cause harm to people's physical and psychological wellbeing. Occupational health and safety laws are thus relevant to workplace bullying.

Various occupational health and safety authorities have developed codes of practice or guidance material to support occupational health and safety legislation in relation to workplace bullying (for example, WorkSafe Victoria 2009; Australian Capital Territory Work Safety Commissioner 2010; Workplace Health and Safety Queensland 2004; WorkSafe Western Australia 2006). Harassment and discrimination are under the domain of anti-discrimination and equal-opportunity laws in Australia.

Occupational health and safety laws are slightly different in the various states and territories of Australia, but the essence is the same: the employer has a duty of care to all employees, meaning the employer must take active steps to ensure the workplace is as safe as reasonably practicable (in both physical and psychological terms), and that each employee is engaged in a safe system of work. Employees also have responsibilities under the occupational health and safety legislation. They must ensure that they take reasonable care to avoid harming others through their acts or omissions at work. Occupational health and safety legislation in Australia typically requires the employer to formally consult with employees about health and safety matters. As is the case in the United Kingdom, cccupational health and safety legislation cannot be used as the basis for civil proceedings in Australia.

A high-profile prosecution for workplace bullying in Victoria (WorkSafe Victoria 2010) has helped put workplace bullying on the radar of employers and employees in Australia. The Victorian government has pledged a major campaign aimed at addressing workplace bullying in that state (Holding 2010).

The South Australian occupational health and safety legislation specifically includes bullying as an area in which employers have a duty of care. The *South Australian Occupational Health, Safety and Welfare Act 1986* refers to inappropriate behaviour towards an employee. Section 55(a) of the Act states:

> *(1) For the purposes of this section, bullying is behaviour—*
> > *(a) that is directed towards an employee or a group of employees, that is repeated and systematic, and that a reasonable person, having regard to all the circumstances, would expect to victimise, humiliate, undermine or threaten the employee or employees to whom the behaviour is directed; and*
> > *(b) that creates a risk to health or safety.*

The same Act also spells out at Section 55(a)(2) what workplace bullying is not:

> *(2) However, bullying does not include—*
>
> > *(a) reasonable action taken in a reasonable manner by an employer to transfer, demote, discipline, counsel, retrench or dismiss an employee; or*
> >
> > *(b) a decision by an employer, based on reasonable grounds, not to award or provide a promotion, transfer, or benefit in connection with an employee's employment; or*
> >
> > *(c) reasonable administrative action taken in a reasonable manner by an employer in connection with an employee's employment; or reasonable action taken in a reasonable manner under an Act affecting an employee.*

The legislation also directs the inspectorate at Section 55(3):

> *(3) If—*
>
> > *(a) an inspector receives a complaint from an employee that he or she is being bullied or abused at work; and*
> >
> > *(b) the inspector, after an investigation of the matter, has reason to believe that the matter is capable of resolution under this section, the inspector may—*
> >
> > *(c) take reasonable steps to resolve the matter between the parties himself or herself; and*
> >
> > *(d) if the matter remains unresolved after taking the steps required under paragraph (c), after consultation with the parties, refer the matter to the Industrial Commission for conciliation or mediation.*

The existence of such legislation notwithstanding, two of the problems in all jurisdictions in Australia are the lack of capacity of inspectors to address workplace psycho-social issues and the resistance of employers to tacking these types of issues (Johnstone, Quinlan & McNamara 2008).

Apart from in South Australia, there are no specific laws pertaining to workplace bullying in Australia and it has not, so far, received specific mention in The Model Work Health and Safety Bill (see below).

There are other laws in Australia that may be used by plaintiffs in relation to the issue of workplace bullying. They include:

- workers' compensation laws;
- industrial relations laws (for example, in relation to unfair dismissal); and
- common law (where damages are sought).

Harmonisation of occupational health and safety laws in Australia

Occupational health and safety legislation in Australia is a matter for the various states and territories and the jurisdiction that covers Commonwealth employees. There are moves to 'harmonise' Australian occupational health and safety legislation nationally, however, in order to ensure uniformity of the legislative framework, including Acts, regulations and codes of practice (Australian Productivity Commission 2010). The Model Work Health and Safety Bill was approved by the Workplace Relations Ministers' Council on 11 December 2009 and is set to commence in January 2012 (Dunn 2010).

Some useful Australian websites

Contact details for the various occupational health and safety agencies in Australia, including 'Comcare', which administers occupational health and safety legislation in the Federal jurisdiction, are given at www.beyondbullying.com.au.

Canada

Regulatory amendments to the national occupational health and safety regulations in Canada were enacted in 2008, requiring employers in federally regulated workplaces to address workplace violence and associated bullying and abusive behaviours (Yamada 2010).

Quebec

Quebec introduced legislation addressing 'psychological harassment' on 1 June 2004 under the Labour Standards Act. To establish that the case actually involves psychological harassment, it is necessary to prove the presence of all of the elements of the definition, including that the behaviours are unreasonably vexatious; repetitive in nature; that there are hostile or unwanted gestures or behaviours; that the behaviours affect the person's dignity or integrity; and that there is a harmful work environment. Under the Act, the employer must put preventive management practices in place. The legislation is enforced by the Commission des Norms du Travail in Montreal (website: http://www.cnt.gouv.qc.ca).

Ontario
The Occupational Health and Safety Act 2007 has been amended to protect workers from harassment, which includes bullying and violence in the workplace. Bill 168, Occupational Health and Safety Amendment Act (Violence and Harassment in the Workplace 2009) requires employers to:

- develop and communicate workplace violence and harassment prevention policies and programs to workers.
- assess the risks of workplace violence, and take reasonable precautions to protect workers from possible domestic violence in the workplace.
- allow workers to remove themselves from harmful situations if they have reason to believe that they are at risk of imminent danger due to workplace violence (Legislative Assembly of Ontario 2009) (website: http://www.labour.gov.on.ca).

Saskatchewan
In 2007, the Occupational Health and Safety (Harassment Prevention) Amendment Act was passed. The Amendment Act extends the definition of harassment to include behaviours that 'adversely affect the worker's psychological well-being' (website: http://www.worksafesask.ca).

France
France introduced the Law for Social Modernisation in 2002 to directly address bullying (Bukspan 2004). It states that 'no employee shall be subject to the repetitive application of moral harassment with the aim to cause, or which results in, the degradation of his working conditions with the risk of damaging his rights and dignity, affecting his physical and mental health or compromising his career' (Bukspan & Hoel 2010). In France, there are

two jurisdictions: one for public servants who comprise 25 per cent of the workforce, and one for those employed in the private sector (Bukspan 2004). The new law makes the following provisions, which are of relevance to private sector employees:

1. No discriminatory measure, direct or indirect, is to be taken against an employee testifying, recording or relating bullying behaviour.
2. The worker who believes they are a victim of harassment presents the judge with supporting evidence, and it is up to the perpetrator to prove that their actions do not constitute bullying, and that their actions are justified objectively.
3. Trade unions can go to court on behalf of the harassed employee.
4. Bullied people can apply to a mediator, and the mediator must be chosen from outside the firm.
5. The State requires the parties to appear before the mediator within one month.
6. Employers must take all necessary steps to prevent bullying behaviours.

Bukspan (2004) notes that, 'compared with the provisions for the private sector employees, the law appears to be much less protective of civil servants and more specifically all those who are employed by public or partly public bodies'. For example, there is no system of mediation provided for the public sector (Bukspan 2004). In addition, a complaint can lead to the cutting of a complainant's income by senior managers without them having to provide justification to anyone for their action in this respect (Bukspan 2004).

The Cour de Cassation (Court of Appeal) developed guides to assist the courts to consistently interpret 'moral harassment', following increased awareness of bullying at work, and a spate of work-related suicides (Bukspan & Hoel 2010). This included that no intent was required to find that moral harassment had occurred. Bukspan and Hoel commented that 'the strength of the jurisprudence recently established by the Cour de Cassation, is that it might encourage risk management behaviour within private organisations'.

New Zealand

The Department of Labour, New Zealand, has published information about workplace bullying in the form of a 'Frequently Asked Questions' publication available on its website. It refers readers to the *Health and Safety in Employment Act 1992*, under which employers have a duty 'to take all practicable steps to ensure that employees are not harmed while at work' (website: http://www.dol.govt.nz/).

Sweden

The Swedish ordinance, known as the Victimisation at Work Ordinance (2003), was the first legal response to workplace bullying (Yamada 2003). It requires employers 'to institute measures to prevent victimisation and to act responsibly if "signs of victimisation become apparent", including providing prompt assistance to targets of abusive behaviour' (Yamada 2010). Hoel and Einarsen (2009) provide a critical appraisal of the introduction of this statutory regulation. The relevant government agency is now the Swedish Work Environment Authority, formerly the Swedish National Board of Occupational Safety and Health (Arbetarskyddsstyrelsen) (website: www.av.se).

United Kingdom

The United Kingdom (England, Northern Ireland, Scotland and Wales) does not have a specific law regarding workplace bullying. However, there are several relevant laws including:

- The Protection from Harassment Act (1997)
- The Health and Safety at Work Act 1974
- Tort and common law
- Contracts of employment

In 2006, Ms Helen Green (Green v DB 2006) was awarded significant damages in a workplace bullying case that invoked the Protection from Harassment Act (PHA) 1997. This Act was drafted to outlaw personal harassment by stalking. Some claims under the PHA, such as the one just outlined, have applied 'vicarious liability to the employer' (Harthill 2008).

Under health and safety and common law in the UK, employers have a duty to 'ensure the health, safety and welfare' of all their employees. The Health and Safety Executive (HSE) include bullying as a workplace stressor (www.hse.gov. uk) and a risk management approach is promoted. The Health and Safety at Work Act 1974 cannot be used as the basis for civil proceedings.

Common law claims may be made if an employer fails to protect an employee against victimisation that has caused physical and/or psychiatric injury (Levinson 2005). If there is a breach of an employment contract which is serious enough to cause an employee to leave, a claim of constructive dismissal may be possible (Namie and Namie 2009).

In 1996, the UK Dignity at Work Campaign initiated a Dignity at Work Bill (1996) which was designed to create 'a statutory right of dignity at work for all employees' (Harthill 2008). For various reasons, however, it was not enacted (Harthill 2008). It has led, nevertheless, to the jointly funded 'Dignity at Work Project' and some organisations have now voluntarily adopted Dignity at Work Policies. As Harthill comments, what is clear 'is the emergence of a social norm that workplace bullying is unacceptable in the workplace'. (website: www.hse.gov.uk and http://www.hse.gov.uk/stress/furtheradvice/ bullyingharassment.htm).

United States of America

Since its enactment, the federal *Occupational Health and Safety Act 1970 (OSHA)* has mainly focused on physical hazards in the workplace. Yamada (2003) argues 'there is little in the statutes and accompanying regulations that will help targets of bullying'. Pioneered by Doctors Namie and Namie, there has been a strong campaign waged in the United States for law reform in respect of anti-workplace bullying laws. In 2000, Professor David Yamada drafted the language of the Healthy Workplace Bill (Namie & Namie 2009). The Healthy Workplace Bill has been introduced (but not yet enacted) in 17 states since 2003 (Yamada 2010). The Healthy Workplace Bill has received a lot of opposition, particularly from employers. However, 'fearing legislation, employment lawyers are starting to advise their clients to adopt workplace bullying policies' (Yamada 2010).

Harthill (2008, 2010) suggests that the USA may have something to learn from the United Kingdom with respect to including workplace bullying in occupational health and safety laws and using existing, but enhanced, frameworks for administering them (websites: www.osha.gov/ and http://www.workplacebullying.org/2010/02/26/bills_alive/).

References

Australian Capital Territory Work Safety Commissioner 2010, Australian Capital Territory workplace bullying guidance material, retrieved 6 April 2010, from www.worksafety.act.gov.au/bullying

Australian Productivity Commission 2010, Performance Benchmarking of Australian Business Regulation: Occupational health and safety, Canberra: Australian Government Productivity Commission.

Bukspan, E. 2004, Bullying at work in France, *British Journal of Guidance and Counselling* Vol 32(3), 397–406.

Bukspan, E. & Hoel, H. 2010, *Bullying and harassment in the French workplace: The evolution of the law*. Paper presented at the 7th International Conference on Workplace Bullying and Harassment, June 2010, Cardiff, Wales.

Dunn, C.E. 2010, 19 March 2010, Undertakings and enforcement of the Model Act, *OHS Alert*.

Green v. DB Group Servs. (U.K.) Ltd., [2006] EWHC 1989 (Q.B.).

Harthill, S. 2008, Bullying in the workplace: Lessons from the United Kingdom, *Minnesota Journal of International Law*, 17(2), 247–302.

—— 2010 The need for a revitalized regulatory scheme to address workplace bullying in the United States: Harnessing the Federal Occupational Safety and Health Act, 78 *University of Cincinnati Law Review*, (4), 101–157.

Hoel, H. & Einarsen, S. 2009, Shortcomings of antibullying regulations: The case of Sweden, *European Journal of Work and Organizational Psychology* 19(1), 30–50.

Holding, T. 2010, Respect at work to help stamp out bullying press release, retrieved 6 April 2010, from http://www.timholding.com.au/2010/02/respect-at-work-to-help-stamp-out-bullying/

Health and Safety Executive UK 2010, Stress: Legal requirements, retrieved 29 April 2010, from http://www.hse.gov.uk/stress/furtheradvice/legalresponsibility.htm

Johnstone, R., Quinlan, M. & McNamara, M. 2008, OHS inspectors and psychosocial risk factors: Evidence from Australia, Working Paper 60, Canberra: Research Centre for OHS Regulation, Australian National University.

Legislative Assembly of Ontario 2009, Bill 168, Occupational Health and Safety Amendment Act (Violence and Harassment in the Workplace).

Lemaire, J. 2009, Bullying: Making the employer manage the risks, *Eric Pearson Study Report*, Sydney: NSW Teachers Federation.

Levinson S. 2005, Resurrecting dignity at work Employment and Human Resources Legalese Special Report, retrieved 1 June 2010 from http://www.manches.com/downloads/SEL_Resurrecting_Dignity_at_Work.pdf

Model Work Health and Safety Bill 2009, retrieved 6 April 2010, from http://www.safeworkaustralia.gov.au/NR/rdonlyres/B62AF65F–9C97–4600-A3E0–8E0D1BA94B9D/0/ModelWorkHealthandSafetyBill.pdf

Namie, G. & Namie, R. 2009, *The Bully at Work: What you can do to stop the hurt and reclaim your dignity on the job*, Naperville: Sourcebooks Inc.

The Health and Safety at Work Act (1974) HMSO, London.

Workplace Health and Safety Queensland, 2004, *Prevention of Workplace Harassment Code of Practice*, Brisbane: Queensland Government.

WorkSafe Victoria 2009, Preventing and responding to bullying at work (3rd ed.), WorkSafe Victoria and WorkCover NSW.

WorkSafe Victoria 2010, Prosecution result summary, Court number Y02114118, retrieved 6 April 2010, from http://www1.worksafe.vic.gov.au/vwa/vwa097–002.nsf/content/LSID164635–1

WorkSafe Western Australia, 2006, *Code of practice: Violence, aggression and bullying at work*. Perth: Western Australian Department of Consumer and Employment Protection, WorkSafe Division.

Yamada, D. 2003, Workplace bullying and the law: Towards a transnational consensus? in S. Einarsen, H. Hoel, D. Zapf & C.L. Cooper (Eds.), *Bullying and Emotional Abuse in the Workplace: International perspectives in research and practice* (1st ed., pp. 399–411), London: Taylor & Francis.

—— 2010, Workplace bullying and the law, 2000–2010: A global assessment, keynote address at the 7th International Conference on Workplace Bullying and Harassment, June 2010, Cardiff, Wales.

part three
TAKING ACTION

Case study: Evan, Part 3

On one of his night call-outs, Evan experienced an unfortunate result that was completely beyond his control. It happens to everyone working in emergency services, and he had experienced bad results before, but it was the first major problem he had encountered since moving to the country. Upon returning to headquarters, Amanda greeted him with a smirk. She had heard about what happened on Evan's job. In Evan's hearing, she commented to Mark that, 'Perhaps the big shot from the city isn't so slick after all . . .' They both laughed. Mark retorted: 'Yeah, they just send us their dregs out here in the sticks. Can you believe they were thinking about making him a manager one day?'

Evan was humiliated by this public lambasting but felt that fighting back would only make it worse. Instead, he simply responded, 'Thanks for your support, guys', to let them know he had heard every word.

What had happened was all Evan could think about. He decided to talk to Bob about the shifts and the remarks that had been made about him, having read the organisation's grievance policy online. The policy was out of date, but it advised that employees should talk to their manager when they had a problem.

Bob had no training in how to deal with the problem. Some training on workplace bullying had been recently made available, but attendance was voluntary and Bob was needed at headquarters. Rather than seeking advice, Bob suggested that Evan should 'toughen up' and asked if he'd like a referral to see the counsellor. Evan was not impressed.

CHAPTER 6: PLANNING AND IMPLEMENTING CONTROLS

We have been discussing how workplace bullying can be a significant problem in workplaces: it can cause damage to individuals, groups and organisations. We've talked about how it can manifest, factors that influence it happening, and how it is different to other types of unacceptable behaviour. The big question now is what can the organisation do about it?

There are a lot of ways of approaching this task, and we need to think about what the organisation can do in a number of different circumstances, such as:

- before bullying occurs;
- while bullying is occurring; and
- after bullying has occurred, and into the future.

The next two chapters consider these points of intervention. The relevance of each will depend on the organisation's size, whether there are current claims, and progress already in place regarding preventing and managing bullying. Some large companies will be ready and able to implement a comprehensive system for dealing with bullying. They will already have some infrastructure and people with skills to develop and administrate such a system. Others will want to troubleshoot their existing system against recommendations. Individual managers may want to develop a checklist of 'what to do if . . .', and targets—or former targets—might want to know what the organisation should be doing in order to challenge them to do so. Accordingly, the information in the next two chapters will enable assessment of interventions at various levels of need.

This chapter is concerned with planning and implementing the organisation's response. It introduces the systems that could be designed and the ongoing processes that need to be considered. We also present a way of prioritising workplace bullying controls to assist in planning the organisation's response. Chapter 7 outlines the issues with designing and implementing complaints procedures because these are consistently highlighted as major problem areas in relation to managing workplace bullying.

Planning the system: The risk management framework

Bullying represents a risk to health, safety and wellbeing at work. In order to comprehensively manage all the risks that can be present in a workplace, organisations use the risk management framework. Indeed, in many juris-dictions, they are required to do so by law. Guidelines on how to implement risk management exist in the form of international standards (for example, Standards Australia 2009).

We don't intend to discuss in detail how to implement a risk management system as there are other sources for this, and many organisations already have this expertise. We are more concerned with how the bullying issue should be incorporated into a risk management system.

The risk management framework has been used very successfully for many types of health and safety risks that organisations encounter, such as manual handling, fire and explosion, and dangerous goods. The incorporation of psychological hazards into risk management has not been as swift or as easy, however, because they are perceived to be fundamentally different to 'physical' hazards. Some of the ways in which psychological hazards are different include:

- their range of effects on health and wellbeing, which is influenced by personal susceptibility;
- their means of identification (including issues of perception);

- their time course (for example, the length of time over which the hazard and its effects occur); and
- the costs of rehabilitation (which are typically greater for psychological hazards than for other hazards, Comcare 2007; see Australian Productivity Commission 2010).

Progress in treating bullying as a workplace health and safety issue is only just beginning. While acknowledged as a health and safety issue, bullying is not yet regarded in the same manner as other workplace hazards for a variety of reasons, including a lack of training and awareness, the perception of it being a 'grey' area, and a general lack of resources for dealing with other 'well-known' workplace hazards (see Johnstone, Quinlan & McNamara 2008). There is hope, however. Other hazards, namely ergonomic hazards, were recently in a similar position, and with persistence have come to be handled more efficiently as health and safety issues. The bottom line is that bullying can be managed, proactively and comprehensively, by applying the risk management framework. Guidance material from health and safety authorities clearly recognises bullying as a health and safety issue, and indicates that bullying should be managed like any other health and safety hazard: with a risk management approach (for example, WorkSafe Victoria 2003, 2009; Workcover NSW 2008).

The risk management approach is conceptualised and presented in several different ways (for example, see Standards Australia 2009), but essentially involves five main steps: planning the system, identification of hazards, assessment of risks, control of risks, and monitoring and evaluation of the system. These steps are complemented by communication and consultation at all stages. Figure 6.1 gives examples of the important considerations at each of these stages.

Risk management has several advantages over less systematic approaches to dealing with workplace bullying. A risk management system is a documented system against which progress can be monitored, audited and evaluated. It provides a road-map to a set of ongoing interventions to prevent and manage risks. Organisations are used to managing risks and many have people with skills and expertise to do so. Administering bullying controls through a risk

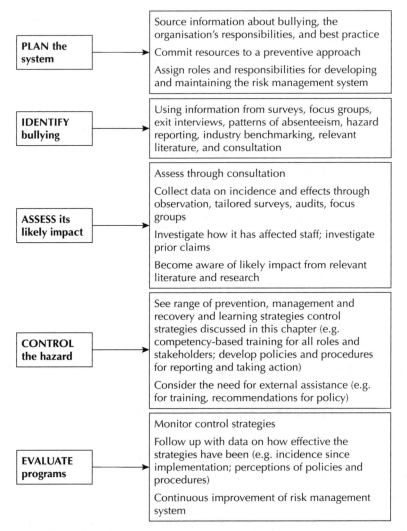

Figure 6.1. Examples of processes at each phase of a risk management system for workplace bullying

management system thus requires an additional focus, rather than a completely new system, which is a major advantage of using the risk management approach.

Though a tailor-made risk management system for workplace bullying takes time to develop, it produces an outcome that not only deals with risks adequately but demonstrates, in and of itself, real commitment to dealing with the problem. Demonstrated commitment is the cornerstone of improved safety culture, and has a range of benefits in employee relations, performance, and ultimately the bottom line.

A well-functioning risk management system also helps the organisation meet its legal requirements and duty of care to its employees. In many jurisdictions, when bullying occurs, organisations and individuals can be prosecuted for breaches of the health and safety legislation—such as for failing to provide a safe workplace, or failing to identify workplace hazards. Therefore evidence that a systematic approach has been taken, with care to prioritise and implement effective bullying controls, may help decrease an organisation's liability should a case go to court. Care needs to be taken when prioritising and implementing bullying controls and preventive programs.

Planning and implementing workplace bullying controls

The complexities and subtleties of bullying make it a little different to physical workplace hazards that organisations are already used to controlling. For 'physical' hazards, we prioritise the control mechanisms we use, from the most effective to the least effective. This process is called applying the 'hierarchy of controls'. Briefly, when following the hierarchy of controls, we first try to *eliminate* the hazard. For example, we remove asbestos from a building, because that is the most effective control for that hazard. If elimination was not possible for some reason, we may *substitute* the hazard with a product that has similar properties but has less potential to cause harm. For example, wool and synthetic mineral fibres have successfully been used as a substitute for asbestos. Alternatively, we might *isolate* workers from the hazard (by creating an exclusion zone around a building containing asbestos), followed by using *administrative* means to control the hazard (such as training people in standard operating procedures). At the bottom of the hierarchy is the use of *personal protective equipment* (such as gloves, respirators and overalls). Personal protective equipment is the weakest option in terms of protection because the hazard is still present. In real situations, a range of controls from several levels are employed in concert to reduce the risk to health and safety presented by a particular hazard, for particular workers.

The hierarchy of controls is not easy to apply to psychological hazards. We cannot always 'eliminate' a psychological hazard, or 'substitute' different people into the workplace or work group. For these reasons, we have developed the time-course model to map effective workplace bullying controls over time (Figure 6.2). The model is based on how prevention, management, recovery and learning strategies relate to different points of intervention relative to bullying behaviours.

- Prevention strategies are those which aim to stop the hazard from escalating into a harmful situation;
- Management strategies, in this context, are akin to 'damage control'. The hazard has already occurred but management strategies attempt to limit the damage before it gets worse; and
- Recovery and learning strategies comprise attempts to restore and strengthen the individual, work groups or organisation after the damage has occurred.

The time-course model can be used as a starting point for evaluating and prioritising the controls that an organisation already employs, or to help identify the control options it needs to develop. In this way, it is a useful alternative to the hierarchy of controls when dealing with psychological hazards at work (such as bullying and other unacceptable behaviours).

The first thing to notice in Figure 6.2 is that prevention, management, and recovery and learning strategies overlap to some extent. Whether a particular control is categorised as prevention, management, or recovery and learning depends to a degree on how it is used in the particular situation (for example, as part of an induction; before or after a bullying episode; as ongoing upskilling or professional development). It is important to note that management and recovery and learning strategies can help inform prevention strategies for the next time the hazard might occur. Indeed, many controls will need to be ongoing and evolving over time in order to be maximally effective. The most important things to remember are that:

- a range of controls need to be used in concert, because any one strategy may be ineffective or incomplete alone, depending on the particular nature of the event or hazard;

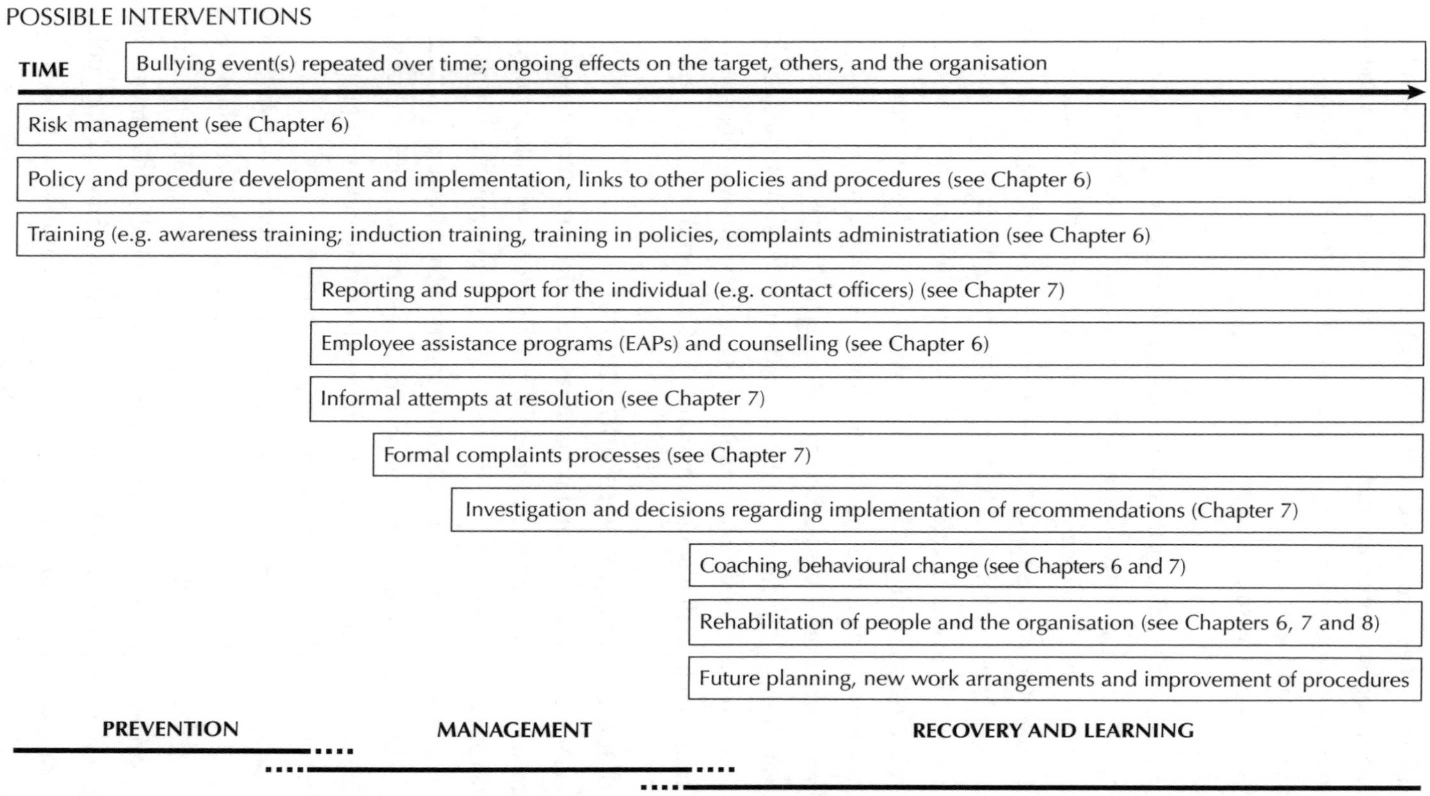

POSSIBLE INTERVENTIONS

TIME   Bullying event(s) repeated over time; ongoing effects on the target, others, and the organisation

Risk management (see Chapter 6)

Policy and procedure development and implementation, links to other policies and procedures (see Chapter 6)

Training (e.g. awareness training; induction training, training in policies, complaints administratiation (see Chapter 6)

Reporting and support for the individual (e.g. contact officers) (see Chapter 7)

Employee assistance programs (EAPs) and counselling (see Chapter 6)

Informal attempts at resolution (see Chapter 7)

Formal complaints processes (see Chapter 7)

Investigation and decisions regarding implementation of recommendations (Chapter 7)

Coaching, behavioural change (see Chapters 6 and 7)

Rehabilitation of people and the organisation (see Chapters 6, 7 and 8)

Future planning, new work arrangements and improvement of procedures

PREVENTION   **MANAGEMENT**   **RECOVERY AND LEARNING**

Figure 6.2. Time-course model of workplace bullying controls. A range of controls should be considered from prevention, management, and recovery and learning strategies.

- provided they are implemented appropriately and consistently, prevention strategies are generally to be preferred to management strategies, and management strategies are generally preferable to recovery and learning; and
- recovery and learning strategies are sub-optimal when used on their own.

Some of the control strategies in the time-course model are quite common in health and safety practice, though they are not always well used. We have become aware of the implementation of control strategies for workplace bullying that can make it appear as though action has been taken, though meaningful action has really not occurred. These are sometimes known as 'tick and flick' interventions, where organisations can quickly prepare a policy, or engage in short or simplistic training, to 'tick off' their obligations without compromising production time or incurring much expenditure. While it is not always easy to gain commitment from organisations to well-resourced comprehensive training and consultative policy development, this should at least be something that organisations strive towards. More information on how and why organisations benefit from quality bullying interventions is in Chapters 3 and 9.

Workplace bullying policies and training

The development of policies and procedures are usually the first steps taken by organisations who want to improve their response to workplace bullying. The workplace bullying policy and procedures (for example, reporting and grievance procedures) should be carefully constructed following meaningful consultation with staff. It is really important that staff 'own' and engage with the policy and procedures. In addition, thorough consultation will mean that the policy is tailored to the particular workplace context.

The policy and procedures should outline the differences between what bullying is and what it is not, and other unacceptable behaviours (see Chapter 2). This is really important in reducing false-positive reporting. This doesn't mean there necessarily has to be separate policy documents, but making an existing harassment policy into a 'harassment/bullying' policy doesn't really do the job unless the policy clearly and consistently outlines the differences between harassment and bullying.

Care should be given to ensuring that the policy and procedures are easily and readily available to everyone. Issues of physical access, language and literacy need to be considered. For example, does everyone in the organisation have access to the intranet, if that is where the policy is located? What about contractors, temporary staff and visitors? Some organisations are moving towards making 'contact officers' available to staff who can help them navigate their way through workplace bullying policy and procedures, in a confidential manner (see Chapter 7).

Most importantly, workplace bullying policies and procedures must be thoroughly implemented. Not implementing policies and procedures is essentially the same as not having them. The existence of an unimplemented policy is not a legal defence, but also, not implementing policies fairly and consistently will cause employees to lose faith. They won't trust the organisation, they won't be committed to the organisation, they won't give of their best. In short, it's bad business all round.

Training is the other major preventive intervention for bullying, however, different types of training can be used as a management or recovery and learning strategy as necessary (for example, retraining following an event). Basic workplace bullying training is usually about awareness: making sure people know what bullying is, and what it's not.

Further, *all* employees must be trained in awareness and policies and procedures. Bullying does not discriminate between roles, tasks and levels, and nor should training. It is imperative for the overall success of workplace bullying strategies that senior management are visibly in attendance at training. It demonstrates commitment, endorses the training and enhances trust from employees.

If particular people have specific roles and responsibilities in bullying policy and procedures, then they need to be thoroughly trained and supported in performing those roles. Line managers and supervisors are often named in policy as individuals to whom employees should report workplace bullying. They are expected to engage in informal and formal resolution procedures, keep information confidential and administer due process. Many people don't even know that they have responsibilities outlined in policy, and are understandably out of their depth when it comes to taking action. This can lead to poor outcomes for all stakeholders, so it is important that people are trained to understand and undertake their responsibilities.

Like all other training, training for workplace bullying must be ongoing, assessed, evaluated and improved over time. Consistent with a risk management approach, a training needs analysis should be undertaken both for individuals and the organisation, and records kept of who has done what kind of training, when they undertook it and their assessment results.

The mode of training that would best facilitate competency should also be considered. There is often a temptation to run training online, though we have found face-to-face training, with facilitated role plays, group work and the opportunity to ask questions to be the most effective.

EAPs and counselling

Many large organisations now employ external providers who supply Employee Assistance Programs (EAPs). The Employee Assistance Professionals Association of Australia Inc (EAPAA 2009) defines these programs as: '*a work-based intervention program designed to enhance the emotional, mental and general psychological wellbeing of all employees*'. The stated aim is to: '*provide preventive and proactive interventions for the early detection, identification and/or resolution of both work and personal problems that may adversely affect performance and wellbeing*'.

EAP services employ clinical psychologists and are paid for by the employer. People may self-refer to the services or be referred by others in the workplace, such as supervisors or occupational health and safety professionals. Individuals are generally limited to a certain number of visits to the EAP service each year. The services are confidential, though de-identified reporting on the number of employees using the service, and the nature of the reasons why they have used the service, are often supplied to the employer to help identify problems areas that require attention at an organisational level.

For many people, the provision of EAP services will be very useful, both for bullying issues and other work and non-work related problems. There have been a number of criticisms of EAP programs, however, regarding how the services are used by the organisation, and confidentiality and conflict of interest issues.

As Rayner and McIvor (2008) point out, EAPs can be seen as a 'cure all' rather than an adjunct to a well-considered and implemented suite of comprehensive interventions. Rayner and McIvor suggest that the use of EAPs can help with parts of the problem, pointing out that: '*while EAPs help specific employees cope, they are generally unable to get to the root of problems (i.e. with the bully, harasser or organisation)*' (p. 23).

Namie and Namie (2009) go further to suggest that it is preferable for people to use independent mental health professionals rather than EAPs. They observe that there may be issues related to honouring confidentiality and a possible conflict of interest because the employer pays the EAP provider's contract. A lack of trust in employer-funded resources can mean that employees go without support, but the organisation could argue that they have taken steps towards satisfying their duty of care (partially), by providing access to such assistance.

Executive coaching

Executive coaching can be employed at several junctures and with several purposes, and can therefore be viewed as a prevention, management, or recovery and learning intervention. Namie and Namie (2009) review that coaching can be used to prepare executives to be more comfortable in confronting perpetrators of workplace bullying, or to educate them on the benefits of preventing and managing workplace bullying.

Coaching the person who has used bullying behaviours is a tertiary strategy, but could be used to limit further harm or as an ongoing personal development strategy following an investigation. It may be particularly useful if the accused holds a senior position and the organisation prefers to attempt positive change, rather than using discipline. Crawshaw (2007) details her approach to coaching executives who have displayed 'abrasive' behaviours. Briefly, it involves three steps: confronting the person with irrefutable evidence of how their behaviours have made others feel; helping them gain insight into how they have affected others; and helping them to learn how to change. As the term 'coaching' implies, while behaviours can be challenged and changed in the future, the development of an understanding of how this can ultimately benefit the individual and the organisation can also be gained (Ferris 2004; 2009). The use of highly experienced and qualified individuals from outside the organisation to facilitate executive coaching is important, considering the potential for defensiveness and manipulation of the coaching situation by alleged perpetrators.

Rehabilitation of people and groups within the organisation

Individuals, groups and organisations that are hurt by workplace bullying often benefit from rehabilitative interventions. These interventions are intended to assist with 'getting things back to normal', including regaining strength, developing strategies for preventing injury in the future, and moving forward in a positive way.

It has been established that targets and witnesses of workplace bullying can suffer from adverse physical and psychological outcomes (see Chapter 3). As well, unacceptable behaviours at work can lead to 'collateral damage', including the ways in which members of a work group relate to one another, and the ways their roles change, which may be a result of someone or some people leaving. Whilst 'rehabilitation' sometimes implies restoring an individual's health following injury or disease (for example via muscle strengthening), rehabilitation in the context of workplace bullying may be required for whole work groups who may have been affected. At such a time, good change management should be practised. This would include provision of rehabilitation strategies, such as debriefing sessions regarding what has happened and how it was dealt with (whilst respecting confidentiality); commitment from all parties in the work group to developing plans to ensure the behaviours do not occur again; and team-building and support strategies.

It may be worthwhile to have an experienced external facilitator assist the group to move forwards. This would help re-establish stability in the work group, and sustain morale and productivity. These kinds of actions are consistent with the risk management processes of monitoring, consultation, communication and continual improvement. Further, these actions are the hallmarks of a learning organisation and an employer of choice.

Other control strategies

Other strategies that are sometimes used for workplace bullying situations are not mentioned in the time-course model. Resilience training is not formally included, because if it is used at all, it should be used with caution.

'Resilience' has become a buzzword in many different fields (for example, business resilience and disaster planning), though with several different meanings. Psychological resilience usually refers to the capacity to move in a positive way from negative, traumatic or stressful experiences (Tugade & Fredrickson 2004). In workplace bullying, and dealing with stressors at work, 'resilience' can be used to refer to making people 'bounce back' after a challenge, make them 'stress hardy' before a challenge, or inoculating them from harm. Strategies that attempt to build resilience in individual employees could arguably be placed in the primary prevention category, however, we have often seen them used after a bullying event has occurred.

Programs that build resilience have been shown to be beneficial. Liossis et al. (2009) showed that a broad-based resilience program that focused on increasing personal resources such as self-efficacy and locus of control was effective in terms of work satisfaction, levels of exhaustion, and work-life balance. In this study, however, resilience was not being used as an intervention specific to workplace bullying.

When used alone as a bullying intervention, resilience training can imply that the individual (target) is the problem, and that if they change their reaction to the situation or environment, then things will be all right. We know how inappropriate and short-sighted this view is from our discussion of all the factors that influence the occurrence of workplace bullying (see Chapter 4). Environmental or contextual factors can often be managed more effectively than individual responses. Using resilience training when organisational or task change would provide more sustained benefits is not only to take an easy way out, but will be less effective and could be seen as a form of 'victim blaming'.

Sometimes it is the content of resilience training that is problematic. Some 'resilience' strategies recommend that targets of workplace bullying befriend the person who is using bullying behaviours, offering them treats or favours. They also suggest that targets should retaliate against the accused bully with smart answers or quips designed to 'block' the bully from further action (Horn 1996; Field 2010). These strategies can encourage a false sense of security because they may work in some situations, but in others they could go horribly wrong. In addition, they can put the target in a subservient position, and imply that it is entirely their problem to deal with. From our discussions so far regarding the organisational and contextual factors involved in bullying, this is a severely limited view.

So, if an organisation is going to use resilience training at all, it needs to be done in the context of other interventions that don't focus on the individual level, and with careful attention to the content and appropriateness of the program.

Workplace bullying is caused by a number of factors and recovery from it requires commitment to multiple interventions, over time. Implementing a comprehensive set of controls in relation to workplace bullying is not easy, but embracing a risk management model can make the administration of such controls easier and more effective. In addition, the time-course model can assist organisations of different sizes and different levels of progress to prioritise more effective bullying control strategies. Central to any workplace bullying prevention system is a reporting mechanism. Complaints and grievances procedures have often been highlighted as an area where things can go very wrong, both for people who are targeted by bullying behaviours and alleged perpetrators. Accordingly, the next chapter considers how to design and implement effective complaints procedures in relation to workplace bullying.

References

Australian Productivity Commission 2010, Performance Benchmarking of Australian Business Regulation: Occupational health and safety, Canberra: Australian Government Productivity Commission.

Brandon, M. & Robertson, L. 2007, Conflict and Dispute Resolution, Melbourne: Oxford University Press.

Comcare 2007, Costs of psychological injury, retrieved 9 June 2009, from http://www.comcare.gov.au/safety__and__prevention/health_and_safety_topics/psychological_injury/costs_of_psychological_injury

Crawshaw, L. 2007, Taming the Abrasive Manager: How to end unnecessary roughness in the workplace, San Francisco: Jossey-Bass.

Employee Assistance Professionals Association of Australia Inc. 2009, What is an Employee Assistance Program? retrieved 5 April 2010, from http://www.eapaa.org.au/

Field, E.M. 2010, *Bully blocking at work: A self-help guide for employees and managers*, Bowen Hills: Australian Academic Press.

Ferris, P. 2004, A preliminary typology of organisational response to allegations of workplace bullying, *British Journal of Guidance and Counselling, 32*(3), 389–95.

—— 2009, The role of the consulting psychologist in the prevention, detection, and correction of bullying and mobbing in the workplace, *Consulting Psychology Journal: Practice and Research, 61*(3), 169–89.

Fox, S. & Stallworth, L.E. 2006, How effective is an apology in resolving workplace bullying disputes? An empirical research note, *Dispute Resolution Journal, 61*(2), 54–63.

Horn, S. 1996, *Tongue Fu! How to deflect, disarm and defuse any verbal conflict*, New York: St Martin's Griffin.

Johnstone, R., Quinlan, M. & McNamara, M. 2008, OHS Inspectors and psychosocial risk factors: Evidence from Australia, Working Paper 60, Canberra: Research Centre for OHS Regulation, Australian National University.

Knox Haly, M. 2008, April 2008, Managing bullying at work, *InPsych, 30*, 14–15.

Liossis, P.L., Shochet, I.M., Millear, P.M. & Biggs, H. 2009, The Promoting Adult Resilience (PAR) Program: The effectiveness of the second, shorter pilot of a workplace prevention program, *Behaviour Change, 26*(2), 96–112.

Namie, G. & Namie, R. 2009, *The Bully at Work: What you can do to stop the hurt and reclaim your dignity on the job*, Naperville: Sourcebooks Inc.

Parker, R. 2008, *The management and operations of the ambulance service of NSW*, Sydney: NSW Parliament Legislative Council, General Purpose Committee No. 2.

Rayner, C. & McIvor, K. 2008, Research report on the Dignity at Work Project: University of Portsmouth.

Standards Australia 2009, Risk Management: Principles and guidelines AS/NZs ISO 31000:2009, Sydney: Standards Australia/Standards New Zealand.

Tugade, M.M. & Fredrickson, B.L. 2004, Resilient individuals use positive emotions to bounce back from negative emotional experiences, *Journal of Personality and Social Psychology, 86*(2), 320–33.

WorkCover NSW 2008, Preventing and dealing with workplace bullying: A guide for employers and employees: WorkCover NSW.

WorkSafe Victoria 2003, Guidance note on the prevention of bullying and violence at work. Melbourne: WorkSafe Victoria.

—— 2009, Preventing and responding to bullying at work (3rd ed.): WorkSafe Victoria and WorkCover NSW.

CHAPTER 7. DESIGNING AND IMPLEMENTING COMPLAINTS PROCEDURES

Many organisations have complaints or 'grievance' procedures which comprise reporting, investigation and delivery of outcomes. Some of these procedures are general and apply to all situations in which a complaint may be raised; fewer are specifically related to workplace bullying. The most important guiding principle behind the procedures should be that of fairness.

Complaints procedures are just one of the management controls that can be implemented (see Figure 6.2), but this step in managing workplace bullying is frequently highlighted as one of the most fraught. Accordingly, we decided to interview a variety of people regarding their reflections on optimising complaints procedures. These people included targets, human resources professionals, clinical psychologists, investigators, lawyers and union representatives. Targets and those charged with implementing the complaints system agree that the (mal)administration of complaints can make bullying situations worse, rather than bring them to an equitable and satisfactory conclusion.

Overview of steps that may be taken in a complaints procedure

The following are the steps, in order of escalation, in a complaints procedure:

1. Seek advice and information from contact officers and/or other sources.
2. Consider self-resolution (see Chapter 8).
3. Make informal complaint.
4. Make formal complaint made.
5. Preliminary investigation
6. Formal investigation (internal and/or external).
7. Determination of outcomes.
8. Internal appeal.

Some organisations set out the steps in a flow chart annexed to the written procedures (for example, see UNSW 2009). An example of a flow chart for an informal complaints procedure appears in Figure 7.1.

There are two fundamental requirements in relation to complaints procedures:

- design—have a high quality, well-documented, step-wise set of procedures in place; and
- implementation—have the process thoroughly, fairly and consistently implemented.

Designing the complaints system

When developing or improving workplace bullying complaints procedures there are a number of important things to consider, including that the procedure:

- includes specific information and interventions for workplace bullying;
- is tailored to the organisation or workplace in which they will be applied;
- is thoroughly and clearly documented;
- is easy to understand;
- allows for accessible reporting;
- requires formal complaints to be put in writing;
- allows for additional support for parties;
- protects all parties involved;
- involves unbiased investigation;

- maintains responsible record keeping;
- pursues fair follow-up of investigation reports;
- allows appeals; and
- includes regular review of the procedure.

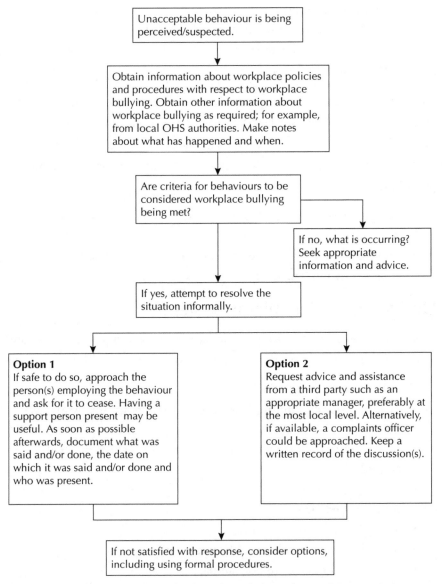

Figure 7.1. Example flowchart of informal procedures for resolving workplace bullying

Specific to workplace bullying

As previously discussed, it is imperative that workplace bullying is managed in terms of its own definition and that it is not simply lumped in with other terminology such as harassment and violence (see Chapter 2). It is acceptable to include bullying in a broad complaints process, but what bullying is, and how it should be managed, should be specifically addressed. The documentation should include a clear definition of workplace bullying and give examples. Of course, in reality, bullying may occur concurrently with other unacceptable behaviours and all the related issues will need to be identified. In complex cases involving multiple types of unacceptable behaviours, an assessment of the most serious issues may need to be made to determine the basis for the complaint.

Tailored to the organisation or workplace

While complaints procedures of other organisations or generic templates can be used as models, they need to be tailored to the organisation or workplace in which they will be applied. Variables to consider include the size, nature, composition and culture of the organisation. It is essential that the procedure is suitable for the organisation in which it is to be applied, and that it has been developed in consultation with employees (and/or their representatives). Resources commensurate with implementing the procedures, such as trained contact officers who can assist staff to navigate the early stages of the complaints, must be provided. Standards promised by the procedure must be reviewed and maintained or improved over time.

Thoroughly and clearly documented

The procedure should be thoroughly documented. It should be clearly written but not cumbersome. A complete set of sequential steps that can be taken should be set out. When it comes to implementation of procedures there should be no element of 'making it up as we go along' because this has the potential to undermine procedural fairness. If the procedure is not explained to all parties, the alleged target can become further demoralised. There can be other consequences including the escalation of the situation or the complainant leaving.

Easy to understand

Complaints procedure documentation should be written in plain language (Asprey 2010). It is a good idea to have a number of people read and comment on the various drafts in order to improve the clarity of the writing. There may also be a need to provide versions in languages other than English, in recorded form and/or in Braille, depending on the composition of the workforce (Lowe 2001). Every employee should have access to the documentation and/ or recording.

Allow for accessible reporting

The procedures of many organisations require that, in the first instance, people who feel targeted by bullying behaviour should ask the perpetrator to cease. Many people who are targeted by bullying behaviour, however, will not feel able to confront the perpetrator. This is quite understandable and, in many cases, it would be inadvisable for the targeted person to confront the perpetrator given the behaviours to which they have been or could potentially be exposed.

Logically, the next step would be to approach the most local manager. Provided that this person is not the perpetrator and does not have a conflict of interest, it is generally expected that a person who considers they have been targeted will take up the issue with their supervisor, team leader or line manager. If reported in the early stages to local management, this may be where the issue is ultimately handled.

This assumes, of course, that the local manager is competent and willing to deal with the report of alleged workplace bullying. It assumes that local managers have been trained and resourced to recognise and handle complaints of unacceptable behaviours in the workplace. The workplace bullying policy should document the expected competencies in relation to the management of bullying complaints.

It may be the case that people have tried internal reporting and they have not obtained satisfaction. Theoretically, the issue can then be escalated to the next level of management and so on. It may, however, be necessary for a person to report outside their usual hierarchical lines (Lowe 2001) or even outside their workplace. There may be a variety of reasons for this, such as fears about loss of confidentiality, fear of reprisal and so on (see Early Reporting, below).

Some organisations, mostly larger ones, have specially trained 'contact persons' often called 'complaints officers' or 'advisers' scattered throughout the organisation. Contact people agree that, outside their normal roles in the organisation, they may be approached for advice. They are not normally involved with human resources management. The role of these people is to listen to the complainants and provide them with information about their options and the resources available to them. In terms of the complaints process, contact officers are only involved at the earliest stage, that is, before a complaint is made. They do not handle or investigate the complaints themselves and they do not represent or advocate for either the complainant or the alleged perpetrator. These people represent the employer. To avoid conflict of interest, they can only relate to one party in the alleged situation. They must be impartial, keep all information discussed confidential and have well-developed listening skills. In the first instance it is most important that people who believe they have been bullied feel listened to (Richards & Daley 2003). The locations and contact details of these people should be widely advertised throughout the organisation.

The selection process for contact people should include recruiting a diverse range of individuals; that is, from a variety of positions in the organisation's hierarchy, in different physical locations, of both genders, and a range of ages. Contact people need to be thoroughly trained and be able to demonstrate a clear and thorough understanding of their role based on the relevant policies, procedures, guidelines and availability of internal and external resources. Contact people must also receive refresher training and be kept up to date with respect to their roles. They may also need to be debriefed in some cases and resources for this should be made available.

As stated earlier, in some cases, it may be necessary for a person to report outside their organisation to obtain impartial assistance. It is early days yet in terms of controlling the workplace bullying hazard and many people are frustrated with the lack of or unhelpfulness of external resources, such as occupational health and safety authorities (Johnstone & Quinlan 2008). Some authors expect that this situation will improve slowly over time (Johnstone & Quinlan 2008).

The consensus among the people we interviewed was that the human resources department (or whatever it is called) is not always a useful place to report. This is mostly because the human resources department is an arm of management and therefore, depending on the situation in which the complainant finds themselves, there may be a conflict of interest. This view is also supported by the literature (for example, Namie & Namie 2009a; Lewis & Rayner, 2003). Rayner and McIvor (2008) reported that people had greater confidence in an outcome where the process of investigation had been conducted in a 'truly independent' way from the start.

Require formal complaints to be put in writing

Most organisations require formal complaints to be put in writing. There may be a specific form used for this purpose, or the person who perceives they have been targeted may be required to write a structured statement or account in their own words of what they believe happened. People with English as a second language or people with limited literacy skills may require assistance with this process. The document, however, should be signed, dated and witnessed as being the true account of the complainant.

There are a number of reasons for this. First of all, as one of our interviewees commented, 'paperwork protects'. It means that the complaint of the aggrieved person is documented and this record of events will be required at various points if the complaint process proceeds. It prevents 'elasticity' of the claimant's case and the process of writing it down serves to focus the complainant on what their issue is about and why they are hurt. It will clarify the situation for other stakeholders, such as the investigator, the alleged perpetrator and, perhaps later, the insurance and legal processes. Obviously, if the claimant has kept records of events over time it will render the written reporting easier for them and it will possibly be more accurate.

Allow access to additional support

It is considered best practice to allow all parties to a complaints procedure to have a support person/people present during proceedings. Depending on the organisation's policy on this matter, this may be in the form of:

- engaging an interpreter where language is a barrier to communication;
- a person with a particular office, such as a union delegate or health and safety representative (if invited by a party to the proceedings);
- advocates or legal representatives; or
- friends, family or professionals, such as a psychologist.

If parties are unaccompanied, a support person should be available should a party become upset.

Ensure protection of all parties involved

The complaints system should include a commitment to all parties being protected from being targeted as a result of participating in the complaints process. Attempts to undermine the complaints process (for example, breaching confidentiality; threatening witnesses) should attract disciplinary action. All the parties need to be made aware of these expectations and responsibilities from the outset of the process.

In some circumstances, organisations allow people to make 'protected disclosures'. This is to ensure that the identities of people who wish to raise a report are protected, such that reprisal is less likely to occur and that matters of concern are more likely to be raised. In these cases the complaint must be made to a nominated officer. Different jurisdictions have laws about protected disclosures; for example, that they are not made vexatiously and they are not made to avoid disciplinary action (New South Wales Ombudsman 2010).

Ensure unbiased investigation

It is beyond the scope of this book to document the exact details of how an investigation should proceed, but the major considerations are outlined. The role of the investigator is to establish the facts of the alleged complaint and then decide, on the basis of the facts and on the balance of probabilities, whether a complaint is upheld or not (Merchant & Hoel 2003).

In some cases it is desirable to use external investigators. It may be the only way for a fair and impartial investigation to be undertaken, particularly in the case of a small organisation. An external investigation will avoid the repercussions of allegations of bias that could result from internal investigations and it could reduce requests for appeals. As well, the use of external investigators may be appropriate in very serious cases or where senior staff members are implicated. Organisations have been litigated against and penalised for conducting complaints processes that have been established as being unfair (Lowe 2001).

There are other advantages, including that suitable outside consultants are appropriately trained and experienced, and they generally have a good understanding of all the legal implications of the alleged situation. Ideally, they will also be experienced in organisational behaviour and methods of alternative dispute resolution and will have no preconceived ideas, conflicts of interest or 'history' with the organisation (Peyton 2003). Large organisations sometimes prefer to develop an ongoing relationship with an external contractor. This enables continuity of service and familiarity with the organisational context, but has the disadvantage of perceived conflicts of interest and bias.

Where external investigators are used, their role, the way in which they will proceed, and how and to whom they will report needs to be in line with the organisation's policy. In addition to this, there should be a documented agreement between the employer who commissions the investigation and the investigator. Also, whether or not the report will include recommendations on actions that can help prevent similar events, as opposed to just a finding relevant to the case, needs to be agreed upon.

Ensure responsible record keeping

Decisions need to be made and documented in polices and procedures about how and where records pertaining to complaints procedures will be kept. All paperwork generated during the complaints process should be stored in a confidential (and perhaps some of it in a de-identified) manner. Depending on the outcome, some of the paperwork may need to be destroyed as an aspect of confidentiality. It is advisable to keep records, however:

- in case the complaints process is challenged or becomes the subject of external investigation or litigation;
- for purposes of data collection, for example, regarding trends; or
- for the purposes of evaluating or auditing the quality of the complaints process.

Such records should be kept in a separate, confidential filing system with access limited to those with a need to know. Only if a person is disciplined in relation to a specific allegation should a record be kept on an individual's file (Lowe 2001).

Ensure fair follow-up of investigation reports

Once an investigation is completed, it is not the investigator's role to implement their report or take part in any disciplinary procedures. It is the role of the recipient of the report (usually the employer) to make decisions about what to do about the findings. The various ways in which this may occur and what other policies and procedures may need to be taken into consideration (such as those relating to discipline and probation) should be listed in the complaints procedure documentation. The decision maker should give reasons in writing for their decision, especially if the decision is not in line with the investigator's findings.

It is assumed that complaints are made in good faith. If it is found that the complaints system has been employed as a means of retaliation or 'payback', then disciplinary action may be taken against the complainant. This should be documented in the complaints procedure.

Allow appeals

An appeals process should be allowed following the implementation of the complaints process if a party is unhappy with the decision. There are various reasons for this including those relating to procedural fairness; for example, where certain evidence was not considered. Appeals reduce the likelihood of people making external complaints or taking further action, including legal action. A time limit during which parties can appeal should be set (Richards & Daley 2003).

Ensure regular review

Regular review of complaints procedures should be undertaken in an effort to constantly improve them. Any new legislation, codes or guidelines that need to be embraced should be documented in the procedures and this list kept up to date. Such documentation should be part of a document control system such that only the most recent documentation is referred to and old documentation is removed from circulation. In addition, planned analysis of the number and nature of complaints, problems encountered in implementation and suggestions for improvement should be undertaken.

Implementation

A bullying complaints procedure will only be as good as the quality of its implementation. If a procedure exists but is not implemented, then effectively, it does not exist. It is simply a document.

Some of the elements that will enhance the implementation of complaints procedures are briefly discussed below. They include:

- early reporting;
- triage;
- accessibility to the process if it has to be taken further;
- effective and efficient gathering of evidence by the investigator;
- thorough awareness of the procedures;
- procedural fairness;
- no conflict of interest;
- timeliness;
- confidentiality;
- thorough training for all stakeholders;
- selection/probation and performance appraisal of those who handle complaints;
- empowerment of those who handle complaints;
- follow-up of investigation reports, including discipline and mediation; and
- monitoring and continuous improvement of the system.

Early reporting

Early reporting enables early treatment to commence if someone has been injured or made ill. Early investigation and implementation of controls can prevent worsening or reoccurrence of the causative factors for either the original complainant or others. Occupational health and safety authorities and those seeking to demonstrate good management practice encourage early reporting of health and safety issues.

Addressing a report of alleged workplace bullying early will hopefully result in less formal procedures being undertaken, which can minimise the impact of the situation on all parties. As one of our interviewees stated, 'Sometimes people just need to download their concerns and know they have been listened to'. Another advantage of early reporting from the point of view of the injured party is that the earlier the reporting is undertaken, the more streamlined any insurance claim process is likely to be.

In the case of workplace bullying there are many reasons why people do not report, do not report early, or even leave their job without reporting the problem. They include embarrassment, fear of losing one's job, fear of reprisal, distrust of the hierarchy, not wanting to be seen as a troublemaker, lack of trust in the complaint handling procedure, low self-esteem, guilt about having possibly encouraged the bullying behaviour and social conditioning (Rayner & McIvor 2008; Namie & Namie 2009a; see also Chapter 3). Trouble-shooting these barriers to reporting is essential.

Employers need to ensure that people are safe and that they feel safe to report what they think are unacceptable behaviours at work. They must be protected from consequences of reporting, such as 'payback' from the perpetrator(s), or supporters of the perpetrator(s), which can be subtly and secretly carried out. The employer needs to ensure this, not simply state it. The absence of payback can never be guaranteed, however. This is another reason why prevention makes things so much easier for everyone.

It is important that the encouragement to report is genuine and not part of rhetoric that masks the true nature of the situation (that is, that reporting is not really welcome). If, in reality, people do not feel comfortable to report then they will tend not to. The nature of the experience that people have when they report will have a great bearing on whether they, or others, will actually report or report again. Word gets around very quickly about how people are treated when they raise 'uncomfortable' issues in the workplace.

We wish to sound a warning about reporting. If reporting is encouraged and people feel comfortable to report, then reports of alleged workplace bullying will tend to increase. This does not mean that the incidence of workplace bullying is increasing; it simply means that reports are increasing. Even though reports will increase where people feel comfortable to report, it is better that people report earlier rather than later or not at all.

Triage

'Triage' is a term often used in emergency medicine in relation to the sorting of casualties. In this sense, casualties are generally sorted in terms of the severity of their injuries or illnesses. The most severe cases are treated earlier and more intensively.

If a person reports that they consider they have been targeted by unacceptable bullying behaviour at work, the first thing to do is to assess how deeply affected they are. You may have to ask them how severe they consider it to be. If, for example, a person is severely distressed and/or depressed then their situation must be attended to immediately. Support must be provided including medical and/or psychological treatment if required or requested. The person should be sent or taken to the facility or professional of their choice, such as their own medical centre or practitioner. It should be remembered that people can react differently to the same set of circumstances. Just because one person wouldn't react negatively doesn't invalidate another person's reaction.

In terms of triage, in less severe cases, a person may state that they wish to informally report an example of unacceptable behaviour. It may not be out of hand and the complainant may not require any further assistance. Nevertheless, the situation should be dealt with as soon as possible and monitored in case it worsens. Lutgen-Sandvik, Tracey and Alberts (2007) use the 'metaphor of being burned by degree'. Their data show that as severity of bullying increases, so do negative outcomes.

The complainant should be advised to keep a diary entry of each and every example of alleged bullying behaviour if it continues and to try and get colleagues to note that the behaviour occurred. This can be very difficult because other people don't usually want to get involved or don't want to become another target of the person(s) employing bullying behaviours. People who are targeted can find this response on the part of bystanders very disappointing.

The next thing to determine in relation to reports of alleged unacceptable behaviours is whether it is bullying, harassment, discrimination, violence, a combination of these things, or something else. This will determine what action is appropriate and enable a decision on what the complaint handler should do.

Accessibility to the process if it has to be taken further

Access to the formal complaints process is the right of every employee of an organisation. The potential complainant should be advised, however, that this does not mean they will necessarily have a good outcome. There is always more to a story than one person's account and no promises can be given to complainants until the full process has been undertaken. For example, the complainant may consider they are being targeted by bullying behaviour, however, a counter-allegation may then be made that the complainant is inefficient and they are not being bullied but repeatedly having their errors or tardiness pointed out.

Effective and efficient gathering of evidence by the investigator

The first thing for the internal or external investigator to establish is whether the alleged behaviour complained about could constitute bullying in terms of the organisation's policy (Merchant & Hoel 2003). If so, any investigation should adhere closely to the organisation's workplace bullying policy and procedures if consequences such as appeals are to be avoided.

The investigator typically interviews the complainant first and any witnesses they nominate. Then the process is repeated in relation to the alleged perpetrator (Merchant & Hoel 2003). A range of other sources of evidence may be consulted, including emails, diary notes, photographs, post-it notes, online social networking records and phone records. Any witnesses nominated by the parties will generally be interviewed on a prioritised basis in terms of the relevance of their relationship with the alleged offence(s); for example, did they directly witness the alleged events or see someone in distress, or can they only provide hearsay evidence? The investigation process can take time and generally takes longer than everyone hopes (see Timeliness).

Thorough awareness of the procedures

Before proceeding with a complaints process, complainants must have the process explained to them in some detail. The complainants should understand what lies ahead for them. It may be the case that once the process is fully explained, the complainant will decide not to proceed. As many people have described to us, the process is 'not for the faint-hearted'.

Similarly, as the process unfolds, others who will be involved, such as the alleged perpetrator, need to have the process fully explained to them. The various parties who will be involved should be encouraged to ask questions and seek clarification about what will happen during proceedings and the wider investigation. The various parties' comprehension of the process on which they are about to embark should be tested to make sure they understand it and the implications of it, particularly in relation to its fairness.

Procedural fairness

Procedural fairness requires that policies and procedures are carried out in such a way that no party is disadvantaged. It means that all parties must be acquainted with how things will proceed and that each party is given an equal opportunity to provide their version of events. As previously discussed, each party must be given the opportunity to seek advice and/or call upon a support person if they wish. For example, it is part of procedural fairness that the complainant must understand that the perpetrator will be told something like: 'It is alleged that on [date] at [time] you [detail the alleged behaviours . . .]'. The complaint must be as fully detailed as possible, otherwise the perpetrator won't have the opportunity to identify what behaviour(s) another person has considered to be bullying. It is meaningless to say, 'You have bullied so and so', without qualification. Specific examples of the allegations should be given.

The people we interviewed stated that people are often surprised that their behaviour has caused offence. It may ultimately be necessary for dozens of allegations to be listed, including each time a particular type of behaviour has allegedly occurred. The alleged perpetrator needs to be carefully assisted to understand that these alleged behaviours are unacceptable in the workplace. This is important for the resolution of the complaint and to discourage repeat behaviours and/or payback.

As part of procedural fairness, the investigator(s) must be impartial. This means the investigator(s) must not be biased or perceived as being biased. If an investigator cannot be impartial, they must withdraw from the process (Peyton 2003). Note that fairness of process concerns the way in which a decision is made and does not guarantee a particular outcome.

No conflict of interest

One of the most important considerations in implementing a complaints procedure is removing conflicts of interest, which have been discussed earlier with respect to the reporting of bullying. The Organisation for Economic Co-operation and Development defines conflict of interest in the following way: 'Conflict of interest occurs when an individual or a corporation (either private or governmental) is in a position to exploit his or their own professional or official capacity in some way for personal or corporate benefit' (OECD 2007).

In the case of workplace bullying, if a person is managing a complaint, they should be certain that they do not have an actual conflict of interest, are not perceived to have a conflict of interest, and do not potentially have a conflict of interest (University of New South Wales 2005). An example of a conflict of interest could be where the person managing the complaint is friendly with one of the parties (either the alleged perpetrator or the complainant). Another example would be where a manager is protecting the best interests of the company rather than allowing a fair process to proceed. We have heard of cases in this respect where human resources managers have been referred to as 'double agents', because while human resources staff appear to be employed to support employees, they are also required to protect the (their) employer (see Lewis & Rayner 2003; Harrington & Rayner 2010). A test for conflict of interest is whether a disinterested person would consider a person's official roles and private relationships do or could at some time conflict (University of New South Wales 2005). If a person considers they do or they may have a conflict of interest, it should be declared at the outset. Ideally, however, actual or perceived conflicts should be engineered out of the complaints process as necessary.

Timeliness

It is important that complaints procedures are carried out as quickly as possible while being as thorough and fair as possible. It is widely known that one of the problems that complainants have with workplace bullying complaints procedures is that they take a long time and progress is often very slow (Rayner & McIvor 2008; Merchant & Hoel 2003). The situation cannot be allowed to fester on and on without some sort of resolution being achieved—that is not good for anyone—but it may well be that things can take a while to achieve. For example, it may take time to contact and interview witnesses. In these cases, the parties should be regularly kept up to date with progress, even where there has been none. In one company we work with, when a complaints procedure is initiated, short, weekly 'update' meetings are held with each of the parties involved, even when there are no significant developments. This reassures the parties that the issue is being dealt with and has not been forgotten, mismanaged, or ignored.

Confidentiality

It is important for all parties to a complaints process to respect confidentiality. This requirement should be emphasised and agreed to by all parties from the outset of the process. Other people should be told only as much as they need to know. All parties should be cautioned against attempting to garner support from colleagues. This is counter-productive, time wasting and polarising.

Careful decisions need to be made regarding what (if anything) will be placed on individuals' files. For example, in many workplaces, only if disciplinary action is taken will anything about the complaint be noted on an individual's personal file. Targets may elect to have the fact that they raised a complaint noted on their file or, on the other hand, they may choose not to.

Thorough training for all stakeholders

As we described in Chapter 6, training of all staff is essential in relation to preventing and managing workplace bullying. The training will vary depending on the position(s) held. There needs to be a general awareness, created through training, of the nature of the procedures and when and how they will be used. It is important that people know how and when to use the appropriate reporting lines. The training should equip people to be able to identify and tell the difference between discrimination, harassment and bullying.

As well, it is imperative that people who are going to be managing conflicts or complaints are competent to do so. This requires sophisticated interpersonal skills that may be underdeveloped in some.

While a lot of organisations are offering this type of training online, our experience shows that it is best facilitated through face-to-face learning, using activities such as role playing followed by discussion/debriefings (Lowe 2001). It is certainly not enough to require people to simply read through policies and be expected to be able to apply them. When the moment comes and a serious complaint is made, that is not the time to try and work out what to do and how to do it. It is like asking a learner driver to be able to drive a car having only read the manual.

People actually need to practise these roles in a 'safe setting' (that is, in relation to a fictitious situation) first. During the first time or couple of times that people manage a conflict situation or a complaints procedure, it would be useful if they were assisted by (or assist) a more experienced person. Useful feedback by way of thorough debriefing needs to be provided in order to consolidate these skills.

Selection and performance appraisal of those who handle complaints

Many managers consciously or unconsciously avoid the 'not easy' issues such as those we are discussing in this book. This is understandable because typically people do not enjoy having to conduct robust conversations or give people negative feedback. It is a significant part of the territory of good management practice, however.

Some managers come equipped to address the issues we have been discussing: they have the make-up and experience to deal with the difficult issues related to people having to work together. Some can be taught these things and learn and apply them well. Frankly, however, some people are not suited to management roles and this should be squarely faced, at least by their employers. Sometimes people are recruited for the wrong reasons. They may be well qualified in their field, technically expert and/ or have significant experience or seniority in the organisation, but they may not have what it takes to make the hard calls required in relation to managing others.

All this implies a number of things. First, it implies that managers are best selected using criteria that will ensure they have the skills and qualities to address the issues we have been discussing, as well as having the technical knowledge to facilitate productivity. Secondly, it means that training and the provision of support resources is required, to varying extents, depending on individual need. And thirdly, it means that some people will not be suited to the role of management.

A rigorous recruitment exercise is required in order that applicants for management positions can establish their competence in terms of people management. The following have been suggested to us as items to be included in the selection process:

- all qualifications should be thoroughly checked;
- applicants could be asked to undertake a handwritten exercise on the day of interview in relation to the position they have applied for and this should include commentary about managing people;

- applicants could be asked for the contact details of a referee with whom they did not get along and for one who was their supervisor in the past; and
- applicants could be asked to describe how they have previously addressed difficult interpersonal situations at work.

Key performance indicators should be set for managers in relation to managing people in conflict, or where unacceptable behaviours occur. Following initial appointment, the setting of a probation period is recommended. During the probation period, performance in all areas of management should be reviewed; not just using a 'tick and flick'-type checklist, but by thoroughly ensuring that standards of performance in all areas have really been met. Comparisons with what was claimed at interview should be made. This will at least reveal any training needs that can be provided while the person is still within the probationary period. Before the completion of the probationary period a detailed performance appraisal will be necessary before a final decision is made regarding the future of the manager within the organisation.

In relation to all of this it would not be considered an adequate approach for a manager to simply 'refer' people to other resources within the organisation when issues of unacceptable behaviours arise. For example, a manager should not be able to abrogate their responsibilities by insisting that one employee lodge a complaint against another employee under the grievance policy and say it doesn't have anything to do with them. Managers should be able to manage these situations, at least initially. It is good practice to build this aspect of professional managerial behaviour into codes of conduct that are promulgated in the probation and performance contracts.

As Graham says (Wyatt et al. 2007), managers should 'lean in' to any difficult interpersonal situations among staff as soon as they are aware of them rather than ignoring them and hoping they will go away. They will not go away. Mostly, they will worsen.

Empowerment of those who handle complaints

People who are charged with handling complaints, as we have already discussed, need to be properly trained and competent to do so. As well, people in this position must be empowered to make certain decisions while handling a complaint. For example, if a complainant cannot face going to work or there is a fear that some form of victimisation may be happening, then the complainant's manager may decide to suspend or relocate the parties for a short period on full pay, or for the period it takes for an investigation to be carried out. Obviously, the complainant's manager would need the power to make such a decision. Various logistical issues may need to be addressed as well. Thus, it may be necessary for a senior member of staff to become involved when things reach a certain point and/or to approve such actions.

Follow-up of investigation reports: discipline and mediation

Depending on the seriousness of the findings of the investigation and the organisation's policy on discipline, there are a number of possible consequences where a claim of workplace bullying is upheld, including:

- warning the perpetrator of the bullying behaviour that it will no longer be tolerated. In this case, the perpetrator's behaviour should be monitored;
- awareness creation/coaching/training for the perpetrator of the behaviour (perhaps with ongoing employment security contingent on outcomes of the programs);
- the establishment of behavioural contracts (agreements on how individuals will treat others, with regular opportunities for monitoring, and/or inclusion in key performance indicators);
- separation of people in place and time so that they do not have to work together anymore (with a warning to the perpetrator). Over reliance on this strategy alone can lead to transferring the problem to a new location, rather than preventing it;
- a demotion or sideways move for the perpetrator;
- changes in duties for the perpetrator;
- non-renewal of the perpetrator's contract; and
- dismissal of the perpetrator from the workplace.

Decisions regarding the consequences for offenders must be consistently applied within the organisation. The consequence should 'match the level of the policy breach' (Lowe 2001). Some people argue that a person who has been found to have perpetrated bullying behaviour should have this noted in their references, though legal advice should be sought before doing this.

Rayner and McIvor (2008) and Knox Haly (2008) have noted a lack of consistency in terms of discipline as a result of complaint processes. Rayner and McIvor (2008) stated that 'certain hard-to-replace employees (e.g. 'creatives') appeared to be protected from sanction'. This was also raised by a number of our interviewees. Obviously, this type of outcome constitutes a further injustice to the aggrieved. If senior managers do not treat offenders, including high performers, consistently, it undermines any anti-bullying initiatives that they have introduced. Where the perpetrator is the most senior manager or owner of the business, the situation can be extremely difficult (Knox Haly 2008) and it is predictable that this organisation is highly likely to suffer high absenteeism and turnover while the situation remains.

A possible injustice has been observed whereby the person who is targeted is the one who is moved. This may represent another form of punishment for the targeted person (Rayner & McIvor 2008). Rayner and McIvor (2008) reported 'unanimous support' for people who raise vexatious or malicious complaints to be disciplined. In cases of conflict at work (see Chapter 2) which have not yet escalated into bullying, mediation may be a useful tool. Mediation is a voluntary process where an impartial third party (preferably a trained mediator) assists the parties to put their respective cases before each other. The mediator's role is to guide the parties towards an agreement with which they can each move forward in a positive way. This is an example of a potentially useful early intervention that may prevent bullying.

On the other hand, where allegations of bullying have been upheld, mediation between the perpetrator and the person or persons targeted is generally not an appropriate intervention. Mediation as a process is designed to assist people in dispute to reach an agreement with which they can both live. Expecting a person who has been targeted by unacceptable workplace bullying behaviour to enter into such a process with their abuser can constitute a form of punishment for the target. In such cases, mediation is not recommended as an intervention for workplace bullying by theorists and practitioners in this field (for example, Ferris 2004, 2009; Namie & Namie 2009b).

Monitoring and continuous improvement of the system

Once a decision is made regarding a complaint, the resolution needs to be carried out and the situation monitored. Ways in which monitoring may occur must be documented in procedures. The reason for this is that monitoring is often neglected or superficial (Richards & Daley 2003). For example, if following the complaints procedure the parties agree to work in the same area, the workability of that arrangement needs to be followed up. Further intervention, such as moving someone or some people to another area, or changing their roles or reporting lines, may be required if problems continue or new problems, such as retaliation, are found to be emerging.

The outcomes of a formal complaints procedure may include re-crediting leave, or an apology (if one is requested and if it can be sincerely given). An apology may be given privately, publically, verbally or in writing. The implications (including legal) of giving an apology need to be thoroughly considered. It can also include an undertaking that the behaviour will not be repeated and periodic confirmation from the complainant that payback isn't occurring. The stakes should be raised if payback does occur and all parties should clearly understand that.

The systems put in place in relation to workplace bullying require continuous improvement. As time goes by, lessons will be learned and the fruits of those lessons should be fed back into the systems as they will apply in the future. One way of monitoring the system is to conduct confidential surveys annually or at specific intervals. Focus groups may be conducted. Other sources of information may include analysis of the results of the staff appraisal system, exit interviews, stress-related absence records (Richards & Daley 2003), anonymous feedback from counsellors, and information from witnesses and whistleblowers.

References

Asprey, M. 2010, *Plain Language for Lawyers* (4th ed.), Sydney: The Federation Press.

Ferris, P. 2004, A preliminary typology of organisational response to allegations of workplace bullying, *British Journal of Guidance and Counselling, 32*(3), 389–95.

—— 2009, The role of the consulting psychologist in the prevention, detection, and correction of bullying and mobbing in the workplace, *Consulting Psychology Journal: Practice and Research, 61*(3), 169–89.

Harrington, S. & Rayner, C. 2010, *Bullying or performance management: Human resource practitioners' responses to workplace bullying.* Paper presented at the 7th International Conference on Workplace Bullying and Harassment, June 2010, Cardiff, Wales.

Johnstone, R. & Quinlan, M. 2008, OHS inspectors and psychosocial risk factors: Evidence from Australia, Working Paper 60, Canberra: Research Centre for OHS Regulation, Australian National University.

Knox Haly, M. 2008, April 2008, Managing bullying at work, *InPsych, 30,* 14–15.

Lewis, D. & Rayner, C. 2003, Bullying and human resource management: A wolf in sheep's clothing? in S. Einarsen, H. Hoel, D. Zapf & C.L. Cooper (Eds.), *Bullying and Emotional Abuse in the Workplace: International perspectives in research and practice* (1st ed., pp. 370–82), London: Taylor & Francis.

Lowe, A. 2001, *Bullying and Harassment*, Sydney: Anthea Lowe and Associates.

Lutgen-Sandivk, P., Tracy, S.J. & Alberts, J.K. 2007, Burned by bullying in the American workplace: Prevalence, perception, degree and impact, *Journal of Management Studies, 44* (6), 837–62.

MacDermott T. 2002, *Managing individual workplace grievances and disciplinary procedures.* Sydney: Australian Centre for Industrial Relations Research and Training, The University of Sydney.

Merchant, V. & Hoel, H. 2003, Investigating complaints of bullying, in S. Einarsen, H. Hoel, D. Zapf & C.L. Cooper (Eds.), *Bullying and Emotional Abuse in the Workplace: International perspectives in research and practice* (1st ed., pp. 259–69), London: Taylor & Francis.

Namie, G. & Namie, R. 2009a, *The Bully at Work: What you can do to stop the hurt and reclaim your dignity on the job*, Naperville: Sourcebooks Inc.

—— 2009b, US workplace bullying: Some basic considerations and consultation interventions, *Consulting Psychology Journal, 61*(3), 202–19.

New South Wales Ombudsman 2010, Protected disclosures, retrieved 2 April 2010, from http://www.ombo.nsw.gov.au/complaints/protectdisclosure.html

OECD 2007, Bribery in public procurement: Methods, actors and counter-measures, retrieved 13 March 2010, from http://stats.oecd.org/glossary/detail.asp?ID=7206

Partnerships Victoria 2005, Disclosure and management of conflicts of interest for advisers, retrieved 30 March 2010, from http://www.partnerships.vic.gov.au

Peyton, P.R. 2003, Dignity at Work: Eliminate bullying and create a positive working environment, Hove: Brunner-Routledge.

Rayner, C. & McIvor, K. 2008, Research report on the Dignity at Work Project: University of Portsmouth.

Richards, J. & Daley, H. 2003, Bullying policy: Development, implementation and monitoring, in S. Einarsen, H. Hoel, D. Zapf & C.L. Cooper (Eds.), Bullying and Emotional Abuse in the Workplace: International perspectives in research and practice (1st ed., pp. 247–58), London: Taylor & Francis.

University of New South Wales 2005, Conflict of Interest Policy. Retrieved 14 July 2010, from http://www.hr.unsw.au/employee/conflict.html

——2009, UNSW staff complaint procedure, retrieved 22 March 2010, from http://www.gs.unsw.edu.au/policy/documents/staffcomplaintproc.pdf

Wyatt, A., Caponecchia, C. & Graham, J. 2007, Beyond workplace bullying [Audio recording]: Beyondbullying.com.au

Case study: Evan, Part 4

Before going to see a counsellor, Evan decided to get more information. He was convinced that he was being bullied, as opposed to being harassed or discriminated against, and it certainly wasn't violence. He found this information after searching online during a slow night-shift. The organisation did have a 'code of conduct' document, pinned to the noticeboard, but no-one ever looked at it. If they did, they would have found that it talked about sexual harassment in part, but focused more on professional conduct and interaction with clients, the public, and other stakeholders. It did not mention bullying, discrimination, or non-sexual harassment, let alone compare and contrast them.

Evan was not keen to raise the issue of bullying at the health and safety committee, particularly given that the chair was one of the people bad-mouthing him. Instead, he decided to phone the regional manager, who informed him that he could lodge a formal complaint. The regional manager insisted that there was little he could do in the short term to improve the shift arrangements. The 'interpersonal problems' Evan was having were a 'bit of a grey area', according to the regional manager. He suggested trying to confront the people involved. Evan related the physical symptoms he was having—headaches, nausea, sleeplessness, anxiety—and the regional manager suggested he took some time off to 'clear his head and adjust to the change'. Evan indicated that he might go to the union, but the regional manager advised against it, 'for your own good'.

Finally, Evan made a confidential formal complaint about the rosters using the organisation's grievance procedure. He attached a great deal of evidence about what happened, including copies of rosters and diary notes of the interactions he had with Bob, Mark, Amanda, the regional manager, and the treatment he received from other staff members. He submitted it directly to human resources.

Two weeks later, some of Evan's co-workers confronted him about submitting the complaint. It was supposed to be confidential. In the tea room at headquarters, Evan was stood over by one of his workmates, while being verbally abused. Under the pressure of it all, Evan broke down.

Evan went on sick leave and applied for a transfer back to the city. He resented being on sick leave and felt useless: he would have much prefered to be working and using the skills he had developed over his career. He was seeing a psychologist and working on feeling better about work and about life in general. He was considering submitting a workers' compensation claim for psychological injury.

CHAPTER 8. THE TARGET'S PERSPECTIVE

What to do

A workplace bullying situation which is not managed generally does not go away—it gets worse and the costs to all stakeholders increase over time (Needham 2003). This chapter outlines what you can do if you suspect or know that you or someone else is being targeted by workplace bullying behaviour. There may be more options than you realise. Before making any premature decisions, such as to leave your job, you may consider the following suggestions:

1. Know your rights.
2. Seek information.
3. Collect evidence.
4. Seek assistance.
5. Look after yourself.
6. Approach the perpetrator.
7. Request informal advice and assistance.
8. Decide what to do next.
9. Be prepared for the possibility of retaliation or for things to get worse.
10. Contact OHS authorities.
11. Use formal complaint procedures.
12. If necessary, appeal the decision.
13. Seek legal advice.

Know your rights

Your employer has a duty of care to provide you with a safe workplace and a safe system of work. You do not have to be exposed to unacceptable behaviours at work. Find out more about your rights and responsibilities with respect to workplace health and safety in your jurisdiction.

Seek information

If you suspect you are being exposed to unacceptable behaviours at work, the first thing to do is become well informed about what may be happening. Find out what workplace bullying is and what it is not. Start by reading Chapter 1 of this book. Various other resources and references are given as well, both in other chapters of this book and in the Resources section at the end. Seek as much clarity as possible about whether what is happening to you may or may not constitute workplace bullying. It may be that what you are experiencing is a combination of unacceptable behaviours including, but not limited to, workplace bullying. If you decide the behaviour is not workplace bullying but is still something that negatively affects you, such as discrimination, harassment or violence, seek more information about those behaviours and about how to proceed. Discrimination in the workplace is unacceptable and illegal, as are some other types of negative behaviours that are described in Chapter 2. Unacceptable workplace behaviours should all be addressed but not necessarily in the same way as workplace bullying. For example, if violence occurs in the workplace it may constitute a crime and it is your right to report it to the police.

Assuming that you consider you are being targeted by workplace bullying behaviour, and it is going unchecked, establish whether or not the workplace has current policies and procedures about it. Gather hard copies of this information where it exists, ensuring that you obtain the most recent versions. In some cases you may find that the workplace does not have this documentation. If this is the case, it is important to confirm the non-existence or the non-availability of this material at your workplace. This is especially important if the matter is to be later addressed by the legal system.

If your workplace does not have such documentation in soft or hard copy, then contact your local occupational health and safety authority for information. Apart from anything else, this information will acquaint you with your legal rights and responsibilities and give you an idea of what your employer should have in place. It will also provide contact details of external agencies that may be of assistance should you wish to report the situation externally. See www.beyondbullying.com.au for links to websites of occupational health and safety authorities.

Collect evidence

Assuming you suspect or are convinced that you are being targeted by workplace bullying, keep detailed notes about what is happening.

In relation to each episode of possible workplace bullying, keep dated, detailed, verifiable (where possible) notes and/or evidence of the following:

- What happened (what was said and done and by whom)?
- When did it happen?
- Where did it happen?
- Who was present? What are their contact details?
- Did you report what happened? How and to whom?
- If you reported the behaviours, what happened as a result?
- How did you feel specifically about what happened? Document your physical and emotional responses, when and where you started having them, and how serious they were. Did these responses change overtime? How?
- Document what you did about these physical and emotional responses (for example, did you consult a medical practitioner; did you try to relax more, or seek social support; did you use particular substances?).
- Document the ways in which your behaviour may have changed at work. For example, are there people or situations that you now avoid? If so, why?
- Can a trend be established? Has this type of event occurred before? How often?

- Does what is happening to you appear to be happening to anyone else, or has it happened to you, or anyone else at your workplace in the past? What information can you gather about this?
- What was going on in the organisation at the time? For example, restructuring, lack of staff.

Keep hard copies of any communication that may be relevant (for example, emails, SMS messages, verbal statements, 'post-it' notes). Always record the date on which messages were received. It is a good idea to keep this information away from the work premises so that you can keep control of it and it can't be copied without your consent or removed from your possession.

It is inadvisable to use the employer's email system to send emails in relation to an alleged workplace bullying situation. Workplace emails may be interrogated and/or deleted. Never send an email in anger, it may be used against you. The last thing a person who suspects or considers they are being targeted by workplace bullying behaviour needs is to be accused of defamation.

Seek assistance

Being the target of workplace bullying can be an emotionally painful experience. While experiencing emotional pain, it is a good idea to obtain support and assistance. Social support from trusted friends and family may be sought. Be careful about seeking support within the workplace unless you are certain those from whom you seek it are trustworthy. And remember that over time, those you seek support from may suffer 'compassion fatigue'.

You may decide to consult your doctor so that your health can be monitored and documented by a professional third party. This will also provide a baseline should things get worse and treatment or referral—for example, to a clinical psychologist—be advisable. You may ask your doctor to provide you with an appropriate leave certificate should you require time away from work. It may also be the case that, should litigation proceed, you may require your medical practitioner to provide evidence.

With any emotional challenge it is often a relief to be able to tell our story to a third party who is trained to listen and can assist you to reflect usefully on the situation. Decisions can then be made about what, if any, are the next steps to take. For example, it may be that in order to obtain relief from a negative work situation, a person may be tempted to leave. This may be a premature or unnecessary move when other solutions can be found which are in the better interests of the person being targeted and perhaps others. In an emotionally charged situation, it is not always easy to see or assess the various options.

You may decide that with some social or professional support you can attempt to deal with the situation yourself, at least in the first instance. You may choose to do this either by speaking with the person perpetrating the bullying behaviour or by seeking support from work colleagues to speak on your behalf or both. Discussing how you might handle the situation with an understanding professional, such as a psychologist, may be useful. You need to consider what the consequences may be for you if you do this, and what further steps you might take, depending on what happens. Being able to workshop ideas about this could be very useful.

Unfortunately, if a person who considers they have been targeted by workplace bullying behaviours decides to proceed with a compensation claim or take the issue to court, there will be more stressors to face. For example, assessment by medical and mental health practitioners will most likely be required. Generally, some 'pathology' will need to be found in order for the targeted person to build a legal case for compensation or damages. In our experience, the findings of a person's chosen practitioner(s) and those nominated by defendants can be discrepant. Some practitioners will find less pathology than others or will attempt to attribute symptoms to pre-existing causes or causes not related to the workplace. This can occur despite the use of practitioner guidelines to quantify the assessments. As one person who was targeted by workplace bullying behaviours commented to us, 'the target has to suffer the humiliation of being "diagnosed" with something in order to mount a case. They never ask for the perpetrator(s) to go through it!'

Undertaking legal proceedings is not for the faint-hearted. There will be many interviews, and you will have to tell your story over and over again, often to people who will be unsympathetic to your claims and/or who know very little about the issues involved in workplace bullying. We offer a few pointers:

- Have all your documentation well organised and summarised so that you can find your way around it easily. Make copies of it. Don't surrender original copies to anyone.
- When attending interviews or consultations, have a support person with you where possible.
- Do not sign anything under duress or if you have any doubts about doing so. Seek advice first.
- Ensure you are aware of your rights under Privacy Laws.
- Be aware that resolution through the legal system, should you pursue it, could take years and may not be successful.

If, after considering your options, you decide to leave your job, there are a few important considerations. We are aware of a number of cases where individuals have stated that one of the biggest regrets they held in relation to leaving their job as a result of being targeted by workplace bullying behaviour was that they had not considered the material costs to themselves of taking such a step.

If possible, ensure that you can obtain a reference before leaving your job, as well as hard copy details of your achievements while working there (for example, certificates gained and evidence of skills mastered). It is also a good idea to seek legal or other appropriate advice about obtaining an adequate severance package should you consider it warranted. This may be especially important if you do not have an alternative source of income or a new job.

Look after yourself

Being the target of workplace bullying can be a miserable experience, to say the least. It is an assault on personal values and can produce intrusive, repetitive, concerning thoughts. In these stressful situations, people are sometimes told to 'look after yourself'. Lists of things one can do to reduce stress at such a time are offered, including 'join a group', 'take up a hobby', 'eat a healthier diet', 'get more exercise', and so on.

Reading such advice and not feeling well enough to follow it can sometimes feel like an added burden. It is common knowledge that if one is miserable, then energy and motivation levels tend to be lower. It is not a time to feel guilty about not joining a gym or taking up other activities—especially if it hasn't been typical of you in the past to do these things. Instead, it is important to do whatever you can do to gently nurture yourself through this time without causing yourself further harm. Exactly what you may do depends on you with respect to your needs, preferences and the availability of resources.

It may be useful to take some time off work if you need it. Ensure you have a medical certificate to cover this. You could use this time constructively to locate and utilise resources that will support and strengthen you.

The time when you are experiencing bullying is not the best time to make big life decisions, undertake very taxing projects, or commit to a large financial outlay. Try to minimise other sources of stress. Do not sign any documents relating to your workplace situation under duress.

A lot of people ask us about self-help groups for targets of workplace bullying. Self-help support groups can be problematic unless the groups are thoroughly facilitated by well-qualified professionals with experience and special interest in the area of workplace bullying. The facilitator's task would be to attempt to move group members in a positive direction in their lives. Where groups are not facilitated in this way, people who consider they have been targeted by workplace bullying will tend to give their version of what happened and that version may be very slanted, subjective and one-sided. The other people listening may sympathise and reinforce the person's outrage (or other negative emotions), which may serve to entrench the problem for the individual rather than provide any workable solutions.

Approach the perpetrator

In the early stages of being targeted by unacceptable behaviour at work, *only* if you consider you can do so, it may 'nip things in the bud' if you approach the person using the unacceptable behavior and ask for it to cease. Several people who have done this have recommended that the behaviour is referred to as 'unacceptable', while others have recommended that it be specifically labelled. For example, you may say something such as, '*I do not appreciate your behaviour towards me when you (nominate what it is that the person does). It amounts to bullying behaviour and it is not acceptable.'*

Be very careful of your tone of voice. Keep it firm and professional. Ensure you speak in a non-threatening way. It is best to not engage in further discussion or get into an argument with the person once you have said what you have to say. Simply communicate that at this point that is all you have to say. Do not give any further information at this time because it will forewarn the alleged perpetrator that you may be thinking of taking matters further and they may retaliate by 'getting in first' with management and complaining about you. If possible, remove yourself from the area and see what happens.

Request informal advice and assistance

In the first instance, it is generally considered appropriate for the person who thinks they are being targeted by workplace bullying to report it informally (see Figure 7.1). The presumption here is 'least said, soonest mended'. Perhaps the situation has arisen for reasons that are quite minor and can be simply dealt with at a local level. It is a good presumption with which to commence even if the case turns out to not be so. Unless infeasible or undesirable (for whatever reason), report to the most local level of management in the first instance and ask for the conversation to be kept confidential. Proceed to more senior levels in the organisation as required—a complaints officer if one is available, or seek advice outside the organisation as and if required. Naturally, if you have a complaint against a person or persons in the workplace and you cannot deal with the situation yourself, someone other than they should be approached for advice and/or assistance.

You may be asked at this stage what you want to happen. For example, the person to whom you report the behaviour may ask if they can talk to the alleged perpetrator, or if they can engage in more formal procedures on your behalf. These actions will depend on the behaviours and local policy, so that's why it is important for you to know the policy first. You may decide that you only want the behaviour to be reported and monitored, in case it gets worse. Asking yourself what outcome you would be happy with could be a useful strategy at this point in the process.

Decide what to do next

At all points along the way you have two major choices: to leave the workplace or to stay. There are many options in between, however, such as asking for the perpetrator to be moved to another area, for new reporting lines for yourself or for the perpetrator to provide certain assurances regarding future behaviours which should be monitored for workability. You may revise your thinking about these things over time. Keep as well informed as possible at all points and attempt to foresee and prepare for the next steps. Constantly reflect on your desired outcomes. Go to all meetings with clear objectives in mind but be prepared to be flexible.

Be prepared for possible retaliation

All the way along, be prepared for retaliation or 'payback' from perpetrators (and possibly their supporters) once you have raised the issue of workplace bullying. The payback may be subtle, not obvious to anyone else (or even you in the first instance). Keep records of anything you consider to be retaliation.

Contact OHS authorities or other outside agencies

Workplace bullying is now officially recognised as an occupational health and safety issue. If workplace bullying goes unchecked, the occupational health and safety authorities can be asked for advice and assistance. Anyone is entitled to contact their local occupational health and safety authority in an anonymous manner. If you have a formal occupational health and safety consultative mechanism at your workplace, such as an occupational health and safety committee, you might like to seek advice from the chair of the committee first. Contact the local occupational health authority later if required. Unfortunately, it is early days yet in terms of the contribution that the occupational health and safety inspectorate can make, but there is evidence that things are slowly improving in this area (Johnstone, Quinlan & McNamara 2008).

Use the formal complaints procedures

If informal reporting does not bring a satisfactory response for you, then formal reporting usually involves communicating the alleged behaviours to the appropriate person or department within the organisation in writing. Best practice formal complaints procedures are described in Chapter 7, and it is a good idea to be very familiar with how formal complaints processes proceed in your organisation. Best practice in relation to complaints procedures requires that they should be carried out:

- fairly;
- impartially;
- confidentially;
- thoroughly;
- in a timely manner;
- by competent people;
- including follow-up of investigation reports, including discipline; and
- including a monitoring and continuous improvement process.

If necessary, appeal the decision

If you are unhappy with the decision that has been reached in your particular situation and/or you consider further evidence has come to light, find out how to proceed to appealing the decision. There may be a time limit on making an appeal. Check this in the organisation's policy.

Seek legal advice

It may be that you need legal advice. If you do not have a lawyer in mind, check with the local law society or association regarding which lawyers take on plaintiff work in cases of alleged workplace bullying. You may also be able to find lawyers who will provide an initial session at no cost to you. If you consult a lawyer, be extremely well prepared and have all your documentation in order. Listen very carefully to the lawyer's advice and take notes rather than spending the time giving the lawyer all the details of what has happened and how you feel about it. A lawyer is not a counsellor.

And after that?

Having been made aware of the occurrence of workplace bullying, the employer should obtain as much information about the situation and manage it in accordance with best practice approaches. This would include seeking information from people who are leaving the organisation—for example, via an exit interview process. Many people, when invited to do so, do not contribute to the exit interview process. If you have chosen to leave the workplace, think about how you might contribute in this respect. You may be able to provide valuable information that will protect others.

When you feel better, you may choose to use your experiences to assist in creating greater awareness of workplace bullying. Visit the many websites about workplace bullying and see if there is something you can contribute. Over time, we hope you will find ways to move on.

References

Johnstone, R. Quinlan, M. & McNamara, M. 2008, OHS Inspectors and psychosocial risk factors: Evidence from Australia, Working Paper 60, Canberra: Research Centre for OHS Regulation, Australian National University.

Needham, A. 2003, *Workplace Bullying: The costly business secret*, Auckland: Penguin Books.

part four

MOVING BEYOND WORKPLACE BULLYING

Case study: Evan, Part 5

Four months later, having found a more senior role in another organisation, Evan had not heard about the progress of his formal complaint. He was still angry about having to leave a job he loved, and that his bad experiences there had not been acknowledged let alone dealt with. He continued to see his psychologist, but was looking forward to a better work life.

Evan's case seems disheartening, but it is based on real experiences from which we can learn. It's important to remember that all cases are different, and that many people will have experienced better outcomes than Evan. Sadly, some have received worse treatment.

Evan was bullied because he was exposed to repeated public criticism and verbal taunts, and he was unfairly assigned to a majority of less family-friendly shifts. These behaviours appear to have been based on envy of Evan's position or skills, and on a cultural practice of assigning unpopular shifts to newcomers.

There were opportunities for intervention at several stages during Evan's ordeal. The first meaningful intervention that was proposed, however, was counselling. Earlier intervention could have included:

- an examination (and reassignment) of shifts;

- training for managers regarding psychological hazards and how to manage claims of unacceptable behaviours;

- updating and implementing codes of conduct, with appropriate training for all staff; and

- staff noticing and acting upon the signs of increased stress and fatigue that were evident in Evan's behaviour and appearance.

Existing procedures could also have been implemented more effectively, including better support from the regional manager, maintaining the confidentiality of Evan's complaint, and timely follow-up of the complaint. In addition, conflicts of interest in the health and safety committee and other roles in the organisation did not help in providing due process for Evan. These conflicts should have been declared and engineered out wherever possible.

Evan's organisation clearly failed in their duty to provide a workplace that was safe and did not adversely affect Evan's health and wellbeing.

CHAPTER 9. MOVING BEYOND WORKPLACE BULLYING

In our consulting work we have been asked, 'Why can't people just come to work and do their jobs? Why does people management have to be so difficult and complicated?' Well the answer is simple. Because we employ people, not robots, and people are individual, thinking, emoting beings.

Managers are paid to manage, and that doesn't mean just getting the job done. It involves demonstrating leadership: inspiring and motivating people while taking into account that they need to work together, and all that that implies.

Bullying is the key workplace health and safety issue of our time. It can affect anyone in any job, regardless of what task they perform, what kind of people they work with, or of what industry they are part. These issues are not easy and they need to be tackled head on, rather than ignored until they become so unbearable for people that they cannot face going to work.

We know that bullying causes significant degrees of harm, and that this harm can be long lasting. Bullying affects not only individuals who are targeted, but their families and co-workers. We know that bullying can take many forms. We know that it can be difficult to prove. We know that it can be a long hard road to recovery.

There are so many misconceptions about psychological variables, including psychological hazards and injury. They are often seen as 'soft issues', as the sole responsibility of the individual, or stigmatised as 'craziness'. Psychological hazards are sometimes seen as too 'variable', in both causation and outcome, to do anything about them. Then there is also the fear that taking action to prevent and control psychological hazards will unleash a flood of similar complaints, and ultimately end in litigation, finger pointing and threatened careers. These perceptions are either baseless, inadequate, or irresponsible. Like other workplace stressors, physical and emotional responses to bullying are diverse, but they are similar enough for us to be confident in our ability to control the stressor. We cannot afford to allow bullying to be dismissed as a 'grey area', or relegated to the too-hard basket. Preventing and managing bullying is a challenge, but it is a challenge that if attempted will reap benefits for all employees and organisations.

Where are we up to with managing this issue?

In terms of research, workplace bullying is a 'young' field. It grew from investigations into schoolyard bullying, and is slowly developing into a rich and diverse field of inquiry. The barriers to the development of this field are significant, and include cross-jurisdictional differences, the translation of theory into practice, and resistance from business groups. Nevertheless, gains have been made in defining workplace bullying and distinguishing it from related unacceptable behaviours. This is a key obstacle that will help pave the way from research to practice.

Government agencies responsible for workplace health and safety are doing more with respect to workplace bullying, but more consistent and meaningful action is required. Safety inspectors generally don't have the requisite resources, training and awareness of psychological hazards, and where they do, their power to take action is often constrained to advice on policy and procedure, which doesn't always help when something has already gone wrong. Greater awareness in the community of unacceptable workplace hazards, along with how to recognise and distinguish between them, would no doubt help focus interventions from safety administrators, and save time in investigating cases that do not represent bullying.

As a health and safety issue, workplace bullying is probably at the point where ergonomic hazards were in the 1990s (Johnstone, Quinlan &

McNamara 2008). Originally ergonomic hazards were poorly understood, and not seen as a health and safety priority. Things are improving, not only with ergonomic issues but many others as well. Similarly, laws and behaviour in relation to public safety issues, such as passive smoking and the wearing of seatbelts, are two examples of where interventions have gradually been accepted over time, and developed into relatively automatic practices.

One of the most significant developments in Australia was the prosecution of workers and business owners for breaches of health and safety legislation following workplace bullying (see WorkSafe Victoria 2010). Not only did this case set a precedent, but it was highly publicised and used as justification for organisations to start taking meaningful action. This much publicised case has been a catalyst for considerable activity at government, industry and workplace levels, similar to major cases internationally (for example, following damages awarded for bullying and harassment at the Deutsche Bank group in the UK; Green v DB Group Services (UK) Ltd. [2006] EWHC 1898 (QB) 1 August 2006).

Bullying is only starting to be fully recognised as an important health and safety issue within workplaces. Many see bullying as a 'conduct issue', or a personality issue that is resolved by intervention at the level of the individual. Hopefully, we have demonstrated that bullying is a systemic issue that requires a sustained systemic response, because it is contributed to by a range of individual, organisational and environmental variables. Organisational variables are inherently controllable. It should come as no surprise that the ways to best prevent and manage bullying are all consistent with good management practice. So better management practices will generally reduce bullying, or, reducing bullying will have the by-product of better management practice. That is a textbook win–win situation.

Of course, that is not to say that improved prevention and management of bullying will ever be easy. There will be complexities and obstacles when tailoring these strategies to diverse organisations. Part of the aim of this book is to convey that prevention and management of bullying is achievable when people at the top are aware, active and committed.

The good news is that we see some organisations shifting towards a new paradigm. This paradigm involves the promotion of workplace-related health and wellbeing while not compromising productivity. These organisations are moving away from performance management followed by punitive interventions when goals are not achieved. They are investing in and valuing wise leaders and managers, not just clever ones or those who have been able to 'stick out' working for the organisation for a long time. In these organisations there is more collaboration towards synergy, encouragement of formal and informal feedback (including negative), greater behavioural integrity and modelled, agreed-upon organisational values. Structural power is not so readily used as a means of control. The managers in these organisations are encouraged and educated to facilitate, coach and support the process of people's ongoing development, rather than simply requiring goal achievement. We predict that less bullying will happen in such organisations along with more growth, loyalty and stability.

How do we move forward?

The first step is increased awareness and myth-busting of the various misconceptions that cloud discussion about workplace bullying. At the same time we need to build commitment and secure people's continuing engagement with the issue. In other words, workplace bullying has to be 'on the map'. This may be contributed to by sustained media attention, taskforces, think tanks, or national awareness days, as already occur in several countries around the world. Robust, peer-reviewed international conferences on the topic, and growing research publications, are contributing greatly to all of this.

As individuals, we can all contribute in several ways. It may be as simple as reflecting on our own behaviour; carefully assessing any suspected unacceptable behaviour; and supporting our colleagues. People who have been bullied in the past, or have witnessed the devastation that workplace bullying can cause, have an important role to play in championing the issue to ensure it doesn't happen again.

Within organisations, we need to refine and extend our existing frameworks in order to better deal with this problem. In many cases, dealing with workplace bullying more effectively will mean an extension of existing documented systems. The infrastructure exists, it just needs the commitment, content awareness and implementation.

Collectively, we can work towards truly making workplace bullying an 'unacceptable behaviour'. Moving values towards condemning these kinds of behaviours is what needs to happen in order for widespread, consistent and long-lasting prevention of bullying. A parallel could be drawn here to how sexual harassment is now viewed in the community. In most places, it is almost taken for granted that any kind of sexual harassment at work is not acceptable. This has been the result of many years of campaigning, increased awareness and societal changes in the roles and relationships between genders. The task of preventing sexual harassment continues, but fostering values that don't condone bullying is essential to progress. Ensuring that workplace bullying is not acceptable anywhere or at any time will have spin-offs for people working in small business where resources to address the issue may be limited.

As a society, we need to provide better resources for targets. This includes information and advisory services, education campaigns, and the provision of truly independent mechanisms for reporting bullying. Our health and safety authorities have a role in facilitating reporting, but other models of managing reports (such as ombudspeople or independent commissions) need to be considered. These efforts to improve support services and reporting mechanisms need to be underscored by laws and compensation arrangements which show an understanding of the complexities of workplace bullying, while providing fair and equitable outcomes for all parties.

Workplace bullying is a complex, multi-caused problem that requires a suite of strategies for its prevention and management. The involvement of many stakeholders will be essential, including employers and industry, unions, lawyers, psychologists, human resources personnel, academics, insurers, governments, and health and safety administrators.

Central to the values of this book is the belief that people should be able to go to work and return home without being harmed. Preventing and managing workplace bullying using a multifaceted approach will substantially reduce the harm that is caused to workers around the world every day, during their normal work tasks. Preventing and managing bullying represents an opportunity for business to capitalise on happy, committed, respected employees. The rewards to business will be enormous.

Moving beyond workplace bullying ensures that work is not just balanced with life, but enriches and fulfils it.

References

Green v. DB Group Servs. (U.K.) Ltd., [2006] EWHC 1989 (Q.B.)

Johnstone, R., Quinlan, M. & McNamara, M. 2008, OHS inspectors and psychosocial risk factors: Evidence from Australia, Working Paper 60, Canberra: Research Centre for OHS Regulation, Australian National University.

WorkSafe Victoria 2010, Prosecution result summary, Court number Y02114118, retrieved 6 April 2010, from http://www1.worksafe.vic.gov.au/vwa/ vwa097–002.nsf/content/LSID164635–1

RESOURCES

Links to relevant health and safety regulators, support sites, and information can be found via the following websites:

AUSTRALIA: Beyond Bullying

http://www.beyondbullying.com.au

USA: Workplace Bullying Institute

http://www.workplacebullying.org/

International Association on Workplace Bullying & Harassment

http://www.iawbh.org/

UK Health and Safety Executive

http://www.hse.gov.uk

UK Advisory, Conciliation and Arbitration Service

http://www.acas.org.uk

APPENDIX

The escalating drama spiral demonstration

Read this case study along with Figure A1.

Repeatedly, over the course of the last month or so, Person A perpetrates bullying behaviour on Person B, by taking credit for things she has done, not informing her of important meetings and subtly excluding her in other ways, such as leaving her address off important emails that she needed to act upon. Person A has also openly criticised Person B's work in front of others.

Person B notices something negative, but doesn't comment at first.

> RED FLAG: First red flag . . . the behaviour is unacceptable and is being repeated.

On two occasions Person C observes Person A perpetrating bullying behaviour towards Person B. Person C does not report it because he fears for his job. Person A is in a position of power, and Person C does not want to rock the boat, even though he knows the behaviour was inappropriate and unfair.

> RED FLAG: Second red flag . . . the behaviour has been witnessed as being unacceptable.

Person B discusses the situation with her partner, Person D.

Person D discusses the situation with one of his friends, Person E.

Over the following week, Person A continues to perpetrate bullying behaviour towards Person B. Person B is now becoming quite upset about it.

> RED FLAG: Third red flag . . . the behaviour, while already repeated over the last month, is continuing, and it is now affecting Person B to a greater extent.

In the tea room one afternoon, when she is feeling particularly low, Person B discusses the situation with her work colleague, Person F.

> RED FLAG: Fourth red flag . . . the behaviour, while already repeated over the last month, is continuing. Person B is affected and has told others about it.

The next day, Person B also discusses the situation (which has intensified to the point where she now cannot get it off her mind), with two of her work colleagues, Persons G and H).

> RED FLAG: Fifth red flag . . . the behaviour, while already repeated over the last month, is continuing. It is now affecting Person B to a greater extent and she is telling more people about it.

Person H suggests Person B discusses the situation with Person I, the human resources manager.

Person B discusses the situation with Person I. Person I tells Person B firstly that it was probably just a misunderstanding. Person B persists, recounting the number of occasions on which the behaviour has occurred. Person I suggests confronting Person A, a prospect which Person B is not very keen on, and is sure will backfire and make things more difficult. Finally, Person I suggests that if Person B can't stand the heat, then she should get out of the kitchen. It is a high-pressure workplace and 'intensive' management behaviour is only to be expected if productivity levels are to be maintained. Person I tells Person B that she can fill in some forms if it was sexual harassment, but that her advice would be to just 'get over it' and roll with the punches.

> RED FLAG: Sixth red flag . . . the behaviour is continuing, and it is now affecting Person B to a greater extent. She has informed the HR manager who has not responded appropriately. This kind of dismissive and unhelpful behaviour occurred at a time when something really could have been done. Someone of authority in the organisation has been approached, and nothing constructive has been done to investigate the possible problems.

Things continue in this vein and Person B starts to become depressed. So does her partner, Person D.

> RED FLAG: Further evidence of effects not only on the target but on others close to the target.

Person B seeks counselling from Person J.

> RED FLAG: Things have affected Person B to the point that she is seeking counselling.

Person J advises Person B to speak with her most senior manager, Person K.

Person B speaks with Person K, who advises Person B that perhaps she 'isn't suited' for high-pressure work and that she should 'seek opportunities elsewhere'. Person K offers to provide a reference. Person K comments that the organisation cannot afford to be without Person A because he is *so productive*.

> RED FLAG: Another opportunity to take the behaviour seriously and investigate further. Indication that the organisation tolerates behaviour because it is in its wider interests to do so.

Person B returns to see Person J.

Person B breaks down in front of Persons G and H.

Person H listens sympathetically and discusses situation (without permission) with Person F.

Person F takes Person B aside and attempts to assist but is not sufficiently skilled to do so.

Person F also draws Persons L, M, N and O into the situation over lunch.

RED FLAG: More and more people are becoming involved.

By this stage, however, the story has changed. Person F relates that she never really liked person A, and that she always found him aggressive and arrogant. She says that, apparently, Person A often yells at Person B on the phone, and that's where it all started. *This was not really the case.*

RED FLAG: Evidence of escalation and misrepresentation which makes the situation worse rather than better; and potentially tarnishes Person A's reputation.

Word gets out that Person B is upset and people take sides, and some of them then change sides to protect themselves. In some circles, Person B is seen as a troublemaker, while in others, Person A is labelled 'a bully'. Other people just don't want to hear about it anymore.

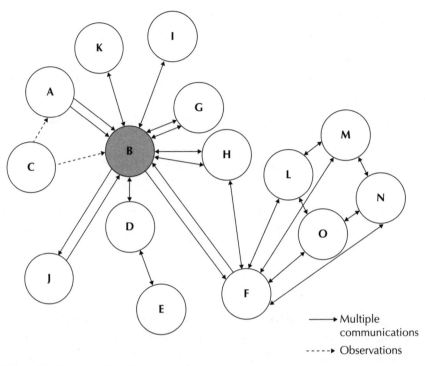

Figure A1: The bullying drama spiral

ENDNOTES

1 High scores on symptoms of PTSD (such as re-experiencing the trauma;
   avoiding stimuli associated with the trauma; and heightened arousal, such as
   sleep disturbance, inability to concentrate) have been found in people who
   have experienced workplace bullying (for example, Matthiesen & Einarsen
   2004). The trauma of bullying is a little different to trauma typically associated
   with PSTD, because the experiences that comprise bullying are cumulative in
   nature, as opposed to single events, such as natural disasters, car accidents and
   so on. With the current diagnostic criteria (American Psychiatric Association
   2000), targets of bullying would not necessarily be diagnosed with PSTD
   (Einarsen & Mikkelsen 2003). Diagnostic criteria for PTSD include that
   the traumatic event involves experiencing or witnessing events that involve
   actual or threatened death or physical injury, which does not always occur in
   workplace bullying (APA 2000).

2 Many personality theorists would not agree with the idea that personality
   cannot change, nor would they support the confusion of personality and
   identity. These are not consistent with contemporary views on the concept of
   personality. 'Academic accuracy' doesn't really matter here, because it is not
   our aim to make people think about personality in the same way as most
   academics. We need to think about how real people in real workplaces are
   likely to view these topics, and adapt our practical approach accordingly.

INDEX